TOP TEN
SINS & STRUGGLES

MIKE MAZZALONGO

Copyright © 2015 by Mike Mazzalongo

ISBN: 978-0692442845

BibleTalk Books
14998 E. Reno
Choctaw, Oklahoma 73020

Scripture quotations taken from the New American Standard Bible®,
Copyright © 1960, 1962, 1963, 1968, 1971, 1972, 1973, 1975,
1977, 1995 by The Lockman Foundation Used by permission.
(www.Lockman.org)

TABLE OF CONTENTS

INTRODUCTION

There are many reasons why people come to church. They come because it's part of their Christian duty; God commands that we not neglect worship:

> not forsaking our own assembling together, as is the habit of some, but encouraging one another; and all the more as you see the day drawing near.
> - Hebrews 10:25

So we make it part of our spiritual practice and exercise. Some come to church for the fellowship; being with other Christians is comforting and encouraging. Others genuinely enjoy the worship and Bible study experience and feel renewed spiritually. These are all perfectly good and Biblical reasons for attending worship services.

However, there are times when the real purpose of our presence at church Sunday or Wednesday is *need*. We need help, encouragement, answers, strength and insight into the problems and struggles we face every day as weak and sinful human beings. Perhaps there is a trouble or illness in our marriage or family; sometimes we feel a sense of loneliness or depression. Our struggle could be a battle with alcohol or any number of addictions. There are many Christians who have to cope with weak faith, discouragement, laziness or negative attitudes. The list of these goes on and on.

Of course, God's word addresses all of these issues. Preachers are eager to help, to comfort, to exhort, even denounce what is evil in our lives, but there is one problem, unlike Jesus who knew men's hearts, modern preachers don't know what's going on in a person's life unless he is told. Unless your preacher knows what the sins and struggles you are dealing with are, he cannot effectively help you with them.

It is interesting to note that people will readily tell their doctors all about their aches, pains and symptoms in order to treat their bodies that will inevitably die. However, they are reluctant to share with their ministers the problems that threaten their souls that will live forever in heaven or hell.

It is for this reason that I have conducted surveys with typical congregations to determine which are the most prevalent sins and struggles in the lives of their members and written this book to address the top ones.

This work attempts to accomplish five goals:

1. Identify the areas where Christians need ministry.

2. Provide teaching from God's word that will address the areas where people have real needs.

3. Help Christians grow in maturity in dealing with sins and struggles, and not just ignore them.

4. Open up the avenue of prayer on behalf of one another concerning our sins and struggles.

5. Provide practical tools from God's word that can be used to win these battles or maintain the struggle against sin without losing faith.

I believe that these are worthy goals and ones that will truly benefit us all.

#10

LAZINESS

In this chapter we'll look at the problem of laziness and how we can deal with this sin in our lives.

> In the beginning God created the heavens
> and the earth.
> - Genesis 1:1

From the very first view we have of God we see Him doing something. In Genesis He is creating the universe.

> [27] God created man in His own image, in the image
> of God He created him; male and female He created
> them. [28] God blessed them; and God said to them,
> "Be fruitful and multiply, and fill the earth, and
> subdue it; and rule over the fish of the sea and over
> the birds of the sky and over every living thing that
> moves on the earth.
> - Genesis 1:27-28

In the first contact that God has with man we see God giving man his first command: to work, produce society and manage the creation. Note that the command to work comes before the command to not eat the forbidden fruit.

We see that from the very beginning God has required mankind to spend energy in work of one kind or another. Even after the "fall" God repeated the command that Adam must work (3:17), except that now, because of sin, his work would be less productive than before. It is interesting to note that neither Adam nor Eve were busy working at the time of the temptation by Satan.

Description of a Lazy Person - Dictionary

The dictionary describes laziness or the lazy person in this way: "..one who does not like to work; one who finds activity or effort distasteful." Let us examine this definition more closely:

1. Does not like that which requires physical or mental effort (work). What are some of the reasons for this attitude?

Immaturity – Some would rather play than work. Some people play and call it work thereby hiding their laziness in play activity or choose to do what requires the least effort.

Selfishness – Physical and mental effort require the giving of self, and a lazy person is basically a selfish one. This is the real problem: a lazy person loves himself too much to give any of himself away in work or service.

2. Laziness loves idleness.

Lazy people love inactivity, sleep, lounging and entertainment more than work. Anything that requires effort or the pain of giving is negative in their experience. Their happiness comes from self-indulgence and easy diversion rather than the satisfaction of accomplishment, effort or service.

Some might say, "This is my life and I can be lazy if I choose to." But the Bible paints another picture of laziness and the true character of the lazy person from God's perspective.

Description of a Lazy Person - Bible

1. A lazy person is wasteful

> He also who is slack in his work
> Is brother to him who destroys.
> - Proverbs 18:9

The lazy person wastes his time, energy, talent and opportunities by not using, under using or improperly using them. Lazy people often invest time into things which are not work, just time fillers. Remember, they avoid work and replace it with activity they like. For example, the file clerk at a company I worked for before going into full-time ministry: she filled her day with busy work to avoid the job she had to do:

- Cleaned her desk
- Put stationary in order
- Talked on the phone
- Long breaks/lunch with pre-break routine
- Wrote birthday cards, shopping lists

She had her day scheduled with these so she could avoid real work as much as possible. She was insulted when asked to do more and requested an assistant. She was fired because her laziness caused her to waste the company's time and money. Lazy people are a burden because they waste other people's time and money since others have to work harder to make up for their laziness.

2. A lazy person is full of excuses

> [13] The sluggard says, "There is a lion in the road!
> A lion is in the open square!"
> [14] As the door turns on its hinges,
> So does the sluggard on his bed.
> - Proverbs 26:13-14

A lazy person is an expert at making excuses: why things should be done tomorrow; why things are not finished; why things are too hard, too far, too complicated, too much, etc.

The reason why a lazy person doesn't succeed is always someone or something else. Usually the lazy ones end up using all of their energy being jealous of others who succeed and blaming them for their own lack of success.

For the lazy person, an obstacle is something which will provide them with an excuse to avoid an effort of some kind. For a diligent person an obstacle is something that forces them to figure out another way of getting the job done.

3. A lazy person is wise in his own eyes

> The sluggard is wiser in his own eyes
> Than seven men who can give a discreet answer.
> - Proverbs 26:16

Lazy people know everything, they know all the answers, you can't tell them anything. But the truth of the matter is that lazy people avoid two things at all costs: effort and truth.

It's a vicious cycle. If they admit the truth (their problem is laziness) they will have to work (make an effort), and they don't like this. So the most effort they make is to avoid the truth.

The Danger of Laziness

Sins are sins because they can harm us in some way or another. Laziness presents a real danger to those who are guilty of this sin:

1. Laziness leads to poverty – Proverbs 6:6-11; 10:4; 19:15

Not just physical poverty but emotional and spiritual poverty as well. Lazy people make no effort for physical things so they won't do it for emotional or spiritual rewards as well.

2. Laziness leads to shame – Proverbs 10:5; 26

A disordered life caused by laziness brings shame on those who depend on you. Those things that bring honor to a person come with effort. A distaste of making an effort brings the opposite: shame.

3. Laziness leads to dissatisfaction – Proverbs 13:4

Eventually one's laziness robs that person of the many joys in life that others have. Lazy people who don't acknowledge the truth grow envious of others and depressed about their own condition.

4. Laziness leads to slavery – Proverbs 12:24

Lazy people still want things but become indebted to others for them. It takes no effort to create debt, but lots of effort to pay them off. So not all poor people are lazy, but most lazy people end up being poor financially, emotionally and spiritually.

And this is not someone else's fault! It is not bad luck, lack of opportunity or talent. It is just plain laziness!

How to Deal with the Sin of Laziness

Enough about the sin itself, let's examine some ways to deal with it. No one is 100% lazy. It is one of the many sins that we all have to deal with at one time or another. Some are more prone to this sin just as some are more prone to anger or sexual sins. However, if this is the sin you struggle with here are some ways to effectively deal with it.

1. Acknowledge the truth

This is the hardest step for any sin - to actually admit that this one is true for us. Nothing that you need in order to help you change will come to you, or be given to you if you do not confess your fault first.

> [8] If we say that we have no sin, we are deceiving ourselves and the truth is not in us. [9] If we confess our sins, He is faithful and righteous to forgive us our sins and to cleanse us from all unrighteousness. [10] If we say that we have not sinned, we make Him a liar and His word is not in us.
> - I John 1:8-10

The forgiveness for the sin itself and all that it has caused, plus the power to overcome it, begins here.

2. Repent

Once you acknowledge the hard truth about yourself you can begin to change. People don't usually change because they either don't know, don't believe or are in denial about the truth concerning themselves. However, if you accept that laziness is really a sin you're guilty of, here are three things you can actually think and do to bring about a meaningful change:

A. Recognize and accept that you have to work.

That you work or make an effort to find work is God's will for you. You're happier and healthier when you obey His will in this matter.

B. Do it now!

Don't put off until tomorrow what can be reasonably done now. Procrastination is the lazy man's effort at working. He sees the task and makes the effort to put it off until later, promising to work tomorrow. The effort will always be made, but in the future. When the future comes the effort is always rushed, at the last minute, sloppy and full of excuses.

Putting off is a habit. It needs to be replaced with a new habit: doing it now. This is true repentance. It requires faith to do things now and not wait until the time is right, or everything is perfect, or you feel like it. If it has to be done - do it now! Repentance from laziness means you have to work, and you should do things right away.

C. Have a Christian's attitude towards the work that you do.

To care for your work and to do it well is a witness of your faith. The purpose of work is not just to counterbalance laziness or provide for our needs, but also to provide for others in need (Ephesians 4:28). We must remember that our work is an offering of service to God, not men (Colossians 3:22-24).

People without Christ see work as a means to an end. I work to produce wealth, power, comfort and satisfaction. Solomon says that here on earth, work is man's greatest source of comfort and joy (Ecclesiastes 2:24). But for the spiritual man or woman in Christ, work is much more than this. For them work is:

- A witness of an honorable life before society.

- An expression of love for one's family as well as those in need.

- A sincere offering of love and service to God in Christ.

A Christian can, in good conscience, achieve riches, power and satisfaction from work, but realizes that these things are not the objectives of work.

Summary

I've said that laziness is a difficult sin to conquer because it is not just a habit (like smoking), it is a character trait. Laziness is a dangerous sin because it can lead to the ruin of our lives and a loss of faith in God. Repentance is difficult, slow and painful, but can be done. True repentance requires:

- Admitting the truth.

- Beginning to do today today's things and not procrastinate.

- A change in attitude about work itself to a more Christian view in order to see it as:
    o A witness of faith
    o An act of love
    o An effort at Godly service

If you repent in this way, God will bless and reward you richly.

#9

ANGER

Let us begin by defining what anger is. It is described as the feeling people experience when something unfair, painful or bad happens to them (Cambridge Dictionary-Online). A strong feeling of annoyance, displeasure or hostility (Google Online). Emotional arousal (Vocabulary.com). I could go on with more sources but all the definitions essentially say the following about anger:

- It is an emotion, like happiness, surprise or sadness.

- It is usually provoked by some negative event. For example, it occurs when we receive or witness unfair treatment, humiliation, surprise, inconvenience, aggression, etc. towards ourselves or people and things we care about.

- It is a strong emotion that can easily lead to other more destructive emotions and behaviors like resentment, hatred, revenge and violence.

Anger is a very common emotion. Everyone becomes angry at one time or another since it is usually the first reaction we seem to experience when facing negative things. For many, however, it is the "go to" emotion whenever things big or small do not go their way. All by itself anger is not a bad thing, it is what anger leads us to do that turns this emotion into a sin.

There are various ways to describe the types of anger that we feel. For example:

1. **Hasty and Sudden Anger:** The impulse when one is threatened or harmed physically or psychologically. A reaction of self-preservation.

2. **Settled and Deliberate Anger:** Reaction to unfair treatment or deliberate harm by another. This is often referred to as righteous indignation or a strong desire for justice.

3. **Dispositional Anger:** Anger as a character trait. A person who is constantly irritable, grouchy and given to having a bad temper.

4. **Passive/Agressive Anger:** This is anger collected and stored from the small slights and insults that some people feel that others are unconsciously directing at them. Their reaction is to sabotage any effort to have or improve relationships as a way of punishing those who offend them.

The first two types of anger are episodic, meaning that they happen from time to time in response to outside stimuli. The third and fourth are always present as part of one's character (not as a response to outside events, but the normal state of that person despite events). No matter what type of anger or how anger is triggered in you, anger is sinful when it becomes the fuel to say and do things which are wrong or hurtful.

Biblical Examples of Anger Fueling Sin

Cain

> [1]Now the man had relations with his wife Eve, and she conceived and gave birth to Cain, and she said, "I have gotten a manchild with the help of the Lord." [2]Again, she gave birth to his brother Abel. And Abel was a keeper of flocks, but Cain was a tiller of the ground. [3]So it came about in the course of time that Cain brought an offering to the Lord of the fruit of the ground. [4]Abel, on his part also brought of the firstlings of his flock and of their fat portions. And the Lord had regard for Abel and for his offering; [5]but for Cain and for his offering He had no regard. So Cain became very angry and his countenance fell. [6]Then the Lord said to Cain, "Why are you angry? And why has your countenance fallen? [7]If you do well, will not your countenance be lifted up? And if you do not do well, sin is crouching at the door; and its desire is for you, but you must master it." [8]Cain told Abel his brother. And it came about when they were in the field, that Cain rose up against Abel his brother and killed him.
> - Genesis 4:1-8

Note that Cain's anger flared up as a result of rejection. God let Cain know that his sacrifice was not acceptable. Anger is a legitimate first response to rejection; we are surprised, hurt and offended. The problem for Cain was how he would respond to this rejection beyond his legitimate moment of anger.

In verses 6-7 God tries to help Cain sort out his feelings by pointing to the reason for the rejection of his offering: he has not done well, there is a sin(s) in his life that renders his sacrifice unacceptable. God warns of the danger awaiting him if Cain fails to deal with this sin. In his case, the anger he felt was a sign that there was something wrong in his life, something he needed to change. We are never told what that was. In I John 3:12 the Bible says that Cain's actions were evil, but not what these actions were.

What we do know is that his anger festered and grew into hatred and resentment of his brother, Abel, whose sacrifice and conduct was acceptable. Repressed anger, left to boil, will soon look for and find a way out. That release is usually directed at some innocent soul who is perceived to be the cause of the anger. In Cain's case God tells him that Cain himself is the cause of the rejection and subsequent anger in his heart. Unable to accept or acknowledge this, Cain targets his brother as the cause of his rejection and ultimately kills him.

In Cain's case, God's rejection and discipline led to anger which gave birth to jealousy which, in turn, created resentment, and this festering resentment drove Cain to murder his brother.

Moses

> ¹Then the sons of Israel, the whole congregation, came to the wilderness of Zin in the first month; and the people stayed at Kadesh. Now Miriam died there and was buried there. ²There was no water for the congregation, and they assembled themselves against Moses and Aaron. ³The people thus contended with Moses and spoke, saying, "If only we had perished when our brothers perished before the Lord!
> - Numbers 20:1-3

Here we see another example of anger and what it can lead to. In this story the cause of the anger was frustration. Moses led the Jewish people out of Egypt as God performed miracles among and through Moses and Aaron, his brother. The Pharaoh eventually let the people go because the miraculous plagues that God punished his country with were crippling it financially and demoralizing the Egyptian population. Moses, despite the fear, complaining, rebellion and lack of faith or gratitude among the Jews continued leading these people for decades. At one time, he even asked God to take him in death in order to save the Israelites from God's wrath because of their complaints and disobedience.

In this episode the people once again complain because of a lack of water and they give in to self pity asking why God has saved them if it is only to bring them into the desert to die of thirst. Moses goes to God in prayer to ask for help and the Lord tells Moses to take the rod of Aaron and go speak to the rock, and water will come forth to provide for the people. In verses 9-11 we see Moses take the rod, but out of anger caused by his frustration, he first scolds the people and then strikes the rock twice with his rod. The water does comes out of the rock but in doing it in this way (striking the rock instead of merely speaking to it as God had commanded him) Moses sinned:

1. He addressed the people in an angry way despite the fact that God had not given him any message to deliver.

2. He struck the rock instead of speaking to it which showed his lack of faith. In Exodus 17:6, in a similar situation, Moses was told to strike a rock once with his rod, and water came forth miraculously. In this instance he was told to simply speak to the rock. That he ignored this command and went back to an earlier method to draw water (striking the rock) showed his doubt. The fact that he then struck the rock twice

demonstrated his further lack of trust in God's word which, as a great leader, was disrespectful of God before the people.

I do not want to belabor the details of how Moses sinned but rather point out to you the ultimate price paid for this disobedience. After 38 years of leading the people in the wilderness, we learn that Moses himself would not enter the Promised Land. Soon after this his brother, Aaron, would die and Moses would spend the next two years preparing the people and Joshua for their entrance into the Promised Land without him.

In his case, frustration led to anger, and this anger led to a loss of faith which caused his disobedience and its resulting punishment.

David – I Samuel 25:2-42

This passage is too long to add here so I will summarize the story (I do encourage you to read it for yourself, however).

Here we have another example of a person experiencing great anger, but in this story we see David avoiding the negative results of this emotion. This episode takes place before David is crowned king and while he and his ragtag army are on the run from Saul (David had been anointed king in place of King Saul by Samuel the prophet, but not as yet recognized by the people). One of the ways that he was building trust with the people was by providing protection from roving bands of thieves and foreign solders who attacked the helpless farmers and shepherds who lived in the country side, far from the larger cities protected by Saul's troops.

One such person was Nabal, a rich businessman who owned livestock. Throughout the year David's men had protected Nabal's shepherds and herders, and at the end of the season David sent some of his men to collect a portion of the flock in return for his services. Notice Nabal's response and David's reaction:

> [9]When David's young men came, they spoke to Nabal according to all these words in David's name; then they waited. [10]But Nabal answered David's servants and said, "Who is David? And who is the son of Jesse? There are many servants today who are each breaking away from his master. [11]Shall I then take my bread and my water and my meat that I have slaughtered for my shearers, and give it to men whose origin I do not know?" [12]So David's young men retraced their way and went back; and they came and told him according to all these words. [13]David said to his men, "Each of you gird on his sword." So each man girded on his sword. And David also girded on his sword, and about four hundred men went up behind David while two hundred stayed with the baggage.
> - I Samuel 25:9-13
>
> May God do so to the enemies of David, and more also, if by morning I leave as much as one male of any who belong to him."
> - I Samuel 25:22

So here we see David's anger kindled by a number of things:

- **Injustice**: he was being denied what was his due.

- **Frustration**: his work would not yield any of the supplies that he needed for the care of his men and their families.

- **Insult**: Nabal dismissed his claim to the throne and referred to him as a runaway slave.

Note that he is immediately consumed by his anger and it leads him to seek revenge. The story then changes scenes and describes what Abigail, Nabal's wife, did to save not only her husband and her household, but also prevent David from committing a terrible sin out of anger. She learns of the situation, prepares the needed supplies that were originally denied David's men, and races to meet the young king before he arrives. Let us read part of her appeal to him:

> [28]Please forgive the transgression of your maidservant; for the Lord will certainly make for my lord an enduring house, because my lord is fighting the battles of the Lord, and evil will not be found in you all your days. [29]Should anyone rise up to pursue you and to seek your life, then the life of my lord shall be bound in the bundle of the living with the Lord your God; but the lives of your enemies He will sling out as from the hollow of a sling. [30]And when the Lord does for my lord according to all the good that He has spoken concerning you, and appoints you ruler over Israel, [31]this will not cause grief or a troubled heart to my lord, both by having shed blood without cause and by my lord having avenged himself. When the Lord deals well with my lord, then remember your maidservant."
> - I Samuel 25:28-31

Note how Abigail diffuses the situation. She apologizes and takes responsibility. She brings the supplies in an attempt to make things right. She acknowledges the insult but warns David about the consequences that would result in his hasty revenge (as king he would have the innocent blood of Nabal's workers on his hands). By asking him to remember her when he becomes king, she acknowledges his true position and submits to it.

We know the end of the story: David accepts her gifts and turns away from his plan. Abigail tells her husband what she did and he dies of a heart attack. Later on, we learn that David marries this rich widow and his food supply problem is taken care of. The story of David and Abigail shows how quickly sudden anger and an immediate response to it can lead to disaster. I believe that the modern phenomena of "road rage" works in this way. One minute you are driving to work and the next you are screaming death threats to a stranger who insulted you with the manner of his driving. Heaven help the situation if you or the other driver has a gun in his vehicle.

Actually, Abigail and David's story provides some good lessons about what to do when provoked to anger, because we cannot eliminate anger from our lives. There will always be situations that cause anger in us. Sometimes God is using our anger (like Cain) to get our attention about something; sometimes it is a sign of fatigue, weakness or misunderstanding (Moses); or at other times a temptation to lead us into sin (David). Prayer helps us to see past the emotion to the cause. Asking, "why am I angry?" often takes the fuel out of the fire. When you find yourself angry, therefore, here are a few things to do in order to deal with this powerful emotion:

1. **Pray:** Note that David, the one chosen by God to be king, did not pray or seek God's counsel before strapping on his sword. Our prayers in such situations should not be to ask God to take away our anger, it should be to seek wisdom and understanding as to why we are angry. What is going on here? Help us, Lord, to avoid a foolish or sinful response to our anger.

2. **Slow Down:** Anger usually causes us to act or react quickly, and say or do things we often regret. Slowing down helps us to get control of ourselves (i.e: it was a good thing David had a long ride to get to Nabal's

house, it gave him time to cool off). I have found that when possible, I will give something that angered me 24 hours to cool off. I usually see things more clearly then and because of this manage a better reaction. You cannot avoid anger, but you can avoid allowing it to create problems if you put a day between the beginning or your anger and the beginning of your response.

3. **Stop "Churning":** If you have prayed, not about the anger but about the cause, and basically have asked God to help you deal with the offense/frustration/injustice/insult, then let it go, stop churning! Churning butter or ice cream means to stir, to mix and to continually agitate. Once you have identified the issue, person or thing that has caused the anger and decided to respond with kindness, or not at all, or with an explanation etc. stop churning the situation over and over in your mind. I know this is difficult, but churning is what keeps the fire of anger burning inside of us. Anger is an emotional prison and the only escape is to let the fire die out naturally by putting a stop to the churning of the details in our minds. Paul says, *"Be angry and sin not, do not let the sun go down on your anger."* (Ephesians 4:26). Paul explains that you can be angry without sinning if you do not prolong your anger beyond its time. *"Not letting the sun go down"* means "for a specific time or season." It is normal to be angry at times, but do not let it go beyond its normal time. To do so will lead to hatred, violence, revenge, resentment, etc. My favorite passage to deal with offense and unkindness/unfairness that stirs anger is Proverbs 19:11, *"A man's discretion makes him slow to anger, and it is his glory to overlook a transgression."*

Be Your Best Christian Self (BYBCS): The hard part about dealing with anger is how to react to the thing that made us angry in the first place. We could spend a long time on this but the short answer is to be your best Christian self. Reaction to insult? BYBCS. Reaction to unfairness? BYBCS. Reaction to frustration, waste, incompetence, etc.? BYBCS. I have found that whatever sin that is at my door, revealed or prompted by anger, I never have gotten into trouble and often have resolved the issue when I tried to respond by being **My Best Christian Self.**

#8

CURSING AND GOSSIPING

It is interesting to note that these two particular sins are tied at #8 and are both sins of the tongue.

Swearing (Cursing)

There are different types of swearing.

1. Swearing as in taking an oath. For example, an oath of citizenship; an oath between two people (marriage); or the personal type of oath described in the Bible where Abimilech swore not to harm Abraham (Genesis 20:1-16). Jesus said to use these type of oaths sparingly (yes is yes, no is no - Matthew 5:37).

2. Then there is the sin of swearing where one uses profanity. For example, using words of a sacred nature irreverently (God, religious things, sacred ideas, etc.), or using coarse ideas or words (of a sexual nature; ugly words describing people or the normal functions of the body, etc.).

Why Do People Do This?

Swearing in public and in the media are common now, but as recently as 1939 you were not allowed to use a curse word in a movie (Gone with the Wind - first movie where the word "damn" is used). The increased appearance of this behavior is a sign of social anger and frustration in people (swearing is the ultimate sign of contempt for others), as well as the rise of a more selfish attitude in American society developing after WWII.

Psychologists tell us that swearing or cursing is a symptom of personal insecurity. It is a way of calling attention to oneself, a self you do not like very much to begin with. This type of language is evident in some forms of popular music which is often angry in nature and displays the attitude of those who produce it. In many of us it is a warning that we lack self-control. Most adults swear when they are angry, some swear to draw attention to themselves and others use this language because of a limited vocabulary. Whatever the reason, swearing never endears us to others, and if we are Christians, it ruins whatever witness we may have for Christ.

Bible Teaching on the Subject

Although there is a lot of bad language in our society, it is not a new problem. Both the Old Testament and Jesus, along with His Apostles in the New Testament, talked about this issue.

> You shall not take the name of the Lord your God in vain, for the Lord will not leave him unpunished who takes His name in vain.
> - Deuteronomy 5:11

This command demanded that we protect the integrity of God's name. His name represented His essence and to defile it was sinful.

> [34]You brood of vipers, how can you, being evil, speak what is good? For the mouth speaks out of that which fills the heart. [35]The good man brings out of his good treasure what is good; and the evil man brings out of his evil treasure what is evil. [36]But I tell you that every careless word that people speak, they shall give an accounting for it in the day of judgment.
> [37]For by your words you will be justified, and by your words you will be condemned."
> - Matthew 12:34-37

What comes out of your mouth is an indication of what is inside of you. Liars speak lies, impure speak impurities, haters of God swear, and good men and women speak truth in clean and encouraging words. I often hear people make excuses for a vulgar and angry person that they know by saying, "down deep inside he is really a good man." My response to this defense is to point out that there is unmistakable evidence to the contrary coming from his own lips.

In Matthew 12:37, Jesus warns that everything we have ever said will be known and judged by God. If this be so, have you ever wondered why we vocally confess Christ before baptism? After all, God knows what is in our hearts, we don't have to express our belief in Jesus out loud for Him to understand. Perhaps it is because God will judge us based only on that confession of faith, and only these words will be revealed about us, the rest will be forgiven.

> Let no unwholesome word proceed from your mouth, but only such a word as is good for edification

> according to the need of the moment, so that it will give grace to those who hear.
> - Ephesians 4:29

Paul tells us not to allow useless words to come out of our mouths (i.e. swearing, cursing, gossip, lies, slander). These things have no worth, produce nothing positive and should not be uttered. On the contrary, the words we do speak should have value. We can know that they have worth because at the moment spoken they build up the people we are with.

> Do not grieve the Holy Spirit of God, by whom you were sealed for the day of redemption.
> - Ephesians 4:30

This passage indicates that worthless speech grieves or makes sorrowful the Spirit of God that lives within each Christian. Useless speech, which is what swearing is, has a destructive effect on everyone: our own self-respect, others in contempt and the Holy Spirit in offense. On the contrary, we should witness our faith with our speech by building others up, and revealing (not hiding) the Spirit of God within us by the things that come out of our mouths.

James 3:2-5 warns against the dangers of the tongue and why we should control it.

> For we all stumble in many ways. If anyone does not stumble in what he says, he is a perfect man, able to bridle the whole body as well.
> - James 3:2

James states that everyone sins with the tongue, it is a common and deadly failing.

> ³Now if we put the bits into the horses' mouths so that they will obey us, we direct their entire body as well. ⁴Look at the ships also, though they are so great and are driven by strong winds, are still directed by a very small rudder wherever the inclination of the pilot desires. ⁵So also the tongue is a small part of the body, and yet it boasts of great things.
> - James 3:3-5

He demonstrates how small things can affect great things. For example: small bits in horses' mouths that control these large animals, rudders that guide mighty ships, and tiny sparks that ignite vast forest fires. These are compared to a few misspoken words that can ruin an entire life.

The Solution - Swearing

> ⁷For every species of beasts and birds, of reptiles and creatures of the sea, is tamed and has been tamed by the human race. ⁸But no one can tame the tongue; it is a restless evil and full of deadly poison. ⁹With it we bless our Lord and Father, and with it we curse men, who have been made in the likeness of God; ¹⁰from the same mouth come both blessing and cursing. My brethren, these things ought not to be this way. ¹¹Does a fountain send out from the same opening both fresh and bitter water? ¹²Can a fig tree, my brethren, produce olives, or a vine produce figs? Nor can salt water produce fresh.
> - James 3:7-12

Bad language, of all types, exists in the world and we hear it all of the time. The solution is to not add to it ourselves and learn to control our tongues. We cannot control others, but we can influence them. In verses 7-12 James tells us that we have the choice of blessing or cursing, but only one instrument with which to do both: the tongue. We need to learn to do one consistently because we cannot do both and be pleasing to God. Continuously producing "fresh water" from our fountains is difficult but possible if we learn to do the following:

1. Control Our Tempers

We need to find acceptable ways of expressing our passionate feelings, and better ways to dissipate negative energy caused by frustration and adversity instead of violent outbursts that include swearing. For example, during these times we can pray, weep, call out to God, sing, run, exercise or talk it out. Having negative feelings and expressing them are fine, but we need to find better and more productive ways of doing this than simply using bad language.

2. Change Our Habits

We need to consciously change our habits of speech and eliminate vocabulary which is vulgar and disrespectful. These include:

- Sexual and bathroom vocabulary (heard among adolescents but not mature men and women).

- Euphemisms: The substitution of a word or phrase for a less objectionable or offensive one.

  - Gee - *"Euphemistic contraction of the name of Jesus."* Webster's New World Dictionary says that Gee is *"a minced form of Jesus used in mild oaths."* We use it as an exclamation or interjection. "Gee, I did not mean it!"

- Gosh - *"Minced form of God, used as a mild oath,"* Webster's Unabridged Dictionary.

- Heavens, Golly, For Heaven's Sake, Gracious, My Lord: All mild oaths using euphemisms for God's name, holy things or concepts.

We may see this as being extreme, however as Christians our conduct and speech should be far above the standards of the world. How can our light of faith shine brightly if we use the very same language as everyone else, especially when it comes to references concerning God and the holy things of our faith?

3. Avoid Temptation

In order to produce good speech we need to avoid people and situations where dirty jokes, gossip and bad language are present. If we find ourselves in this situation it will require true courage and conviction as well as self-discipline to change the course of a conversation that is going the wrong way. Sometimes we need to simply walk away.

4. Acknowledge the Failing

Some may note a Christian's offense at bad language and think, "He's not going to tell me how to talk" or, "You are being self-righteous and over zealous in this matter." We cannot produce pure, clear and fresh communication unless we understand and acknowledge that we (or others in our circle) are wrong and may have been so for years on this matter. We need to learn to say, "I have used bad/offensive language" and apologize for it when we lose our temper or unwisely tell a story that uses vulgar or coarse language. Learning to acknowledge to God and others that we have used poor language and intend to do better is the first step in gaining self-control.

5. Fly With Eagles

The old adage, "If you want to fly like an eagle, don't hang around with the chickens" is true when referring to the use of bad language. We have to develop friendships and habits that create a building atmosphere if we want to affect real change. This means avoiding people who spend all their time complaining, swearing and gossiping. Spiritual wisdom leads us to drink from the fountain of those who have pure water and in doing so we will eventually produce clean water as well.

Summary I

Swearing is the use of coarse language and the improper use of sacred names or concepts in our everyday communication. People swear for various reasons but usually because of frustration, lack of self-control, low self-esteem, ignorance or immaturity. The Bible teaches us that what comes out of our mouths is an indication of what is in our hearts, and one way to purify our hearts is to guard carefully what comes out of our mouths because we will be judged for this.

> Set a guard, O Lord, over my mouth;
> Keep watch over the door of my lips.
> - Psalms 141:3

The best way to avoid swearing and evil communication is to experience the joy that comes from saying what is right and good as well as hearing it said to us.

GOSSIP

Butch Adams (mydailypause.org) says that gossip is a sin because it goes against both the basic command to love our neighbor and the direct command from Jesus as Christians to especially love the brethren. Gossip is the revealing and sharing of negative things about others. This type of communication is gossip because it is done without the person in question's knowledge or permission, and usually shared without confirmed facts. Speech is gossip when you reveal or share what you know is true concerning a negative thing about another. Speech is malicious gossip when what you share is based simply on rumor and innuendo, and meant to harm.

Either way, gossip harms everybody involved: the source of the gossip betrays a confidence or is guilty of spreading a hurtful truth or a damaging lie about another; the carriers are hurt because they share in the original sin and contribute to its amplification; the victim is hurt because whether the information is true or not, a negative thing is attributed to them which they will have to bear from now on. The damage caused by gossip can rarely be undone. Gossip, therefore, is a serious sin because it violates the basic command to love one another, does serious damage to many people and is not easily repaired.

Gossip and the Bible

At least three of the New Testament writers teach us about this sin; a sign that this is a common problem among believers.

Paul the Apostle

> [29]Let no unwholesome word proceed from your mouth, but only such a word as is good for edification according to the need of the moment, so that it will give grace to those who hear. [30]Do not grieve the Holy Spirit of God, by whom you were sealed for the day of redemption. [31]Let all bitterness and wrath and anger and clamor and slander be put away from you, along with all malice.
> - Ephesians 4:29-31

Note that Paul includes gossip (slander) in the same category as anger, malice, wrath and bitterness. It is interesting that in this verse the conjugation "and" is used to link all of these words suggesting that they are equal in their degree of wrongness and potential for harm. Paul says that Christians should put this kind of speech away from themselves.

> [11]Do not speak against one another, brethren. He who speaks against a brother or judges his brother, speaks against the law and judges the law; but if you judge the law, you are not a doer of the law but a judge of it. [12]There is only one Lawgiver and Judge, the One who is able to save and to destroy; but who are you who judge your neighbor?
> - James 4:11-12

Gossip has an element of judgment in it since we not only pass along the failings or foolishness of others, we also render a silent judgment of them as well. In this context James asks, "Who are you to judge another person by making known their weaknesses or criticizing them?" Only God can judge because He is without sin, knows the Law perfectly and also knows the individual completely, therefore

His judgment is perfect. Criticism and the gossip that surrounds it tend to put the gossiper in the role of judge, a position only God has a right and the ability to fulfill. Even courtroom judges have to qualify for their positions and are guided by laws as well as the rules of evidence so as to not be influenced by hearsay (gossip) or rumors. They are supposed to judge impartially according to proven facts and the rules of law, things that are usually absent when people engage in gossip.

Peter the Apostle

> Therefore, putting aside all malice and all deceit and hypocrisy and envy and all slander
> - I Peter 2:1

Peter echoes Paul's instruction to put aside this type of speech but adds the idea that the reason we do these things is because we like it and desire to hear and traffic in gossip. For example, "Have I got a story for you!" This common phrase that often precedes some type of gossip suggests that both the speaker and the trafficker in the gossip enjoy and relish the experience.

Peter's admonition is to cultivate a desire for the spiritual nourishment that comes from God's word, like babies are anxious for their mother's milk ("pure milk") and not the toxic mix of hearsay, hypocrisy and the envy that is often the motivating factor for gossip in the first place. For example, "Have you heard? Betty bought a new car. Her other one was only five years old. Must be nice being a lawyer's wife!"

Unlike gossip, the motivation for feeding on God's word is the fact that it was through this Word that we learned of Christ and His sacrifice for us. How can we accept and enjoy this gift and participate in destructive gossip at the same time?

The Solution – Gossip

Like every sin and bad habit, the solution requires effort and the practice of different kinds of speech. Here are a few things to learn in order to deal with the sin of gossip:

1. Learn to Apologize

> A man's pride will bring him low,
> But a humble spirit will obtain honor.
> - Proverbs 29:23

If you sin with your tongue, repent with your tongue. Apologize to the one you have gossiped about as well as the one you have drawn into sin by gossiping with. This will discourage the desire to receive or traffic in gossip in the future, and will be a painful yet effective way to cultivate humility and cut down on gossip in your own life. Do this a couple of times and I assure you that people will not want to share gossip with you.

2. Learn to Hold Your Tongue

> When there are many words, transgression is unavoidable,
> But he who restrains his lips is wise.
> - Proverbs 10:19
>
> Even a fool, when he keeps silent, is considered wise;
> When he closes his lips, he is considered prudent.
> - Proverbs 17:28

MIKE MAZZALONGO | 39

There is usually not much left to say if we eliminate what is untrue, exaggerated, distorted, unnecessary, coarse, repetitious, hurtful or stupid. We do not always have to say everything that passes through our minds or reported to us by someone else. Doing so is a form of pride.

> A fool does not delight in understanding,
> But only in revealing his own mind.
> - Proverbs 18:2

Learn to filter what comes into our hearts and goes out of our mouths through the spiritual quality control provided us by God's word.

> [8]Finally, brethren, whatever is true, whatever is honorable, whatever is right, whatever is pure, whatever is lovely, whatever is of good repute, if there is any excellence and if anything worthy of praise, dwell on these things. [9]The things you have learned and received and heard and seen in me, practice these things, and the God of peace will be with you.
> - Philippians 4:8-9

Note that the reward for correctly filtering and processing the things we hear, say or repeat is peace, the exact opposite of what is produced by gossip.

3. Learn How to Say the Right Thing at the Right Time

> The wise in heart will be called understanding,
> And sweetness of speech increases persuasiveness.
> - Proverbs 16:21

> Like apples of gold in settings of silver
> Is a word spoken in right circumstances.
> - Proverbs 25:11

God has given us the ability to speak in order to praise Him, express ourselves, and communicate and bless one another. It takes time and practice but we need to consciously learn to do these things in a wise and gracious way. As Christians we do not always have an opportunity to use our speech to confess Christ, but if our speech is coarse, foolish and full of gossip, no one will take our witness for the Lord seriously when that moment comes. You see, not only God judges us for what comes out of our mouths, our brethren and non-belivers do as well.

Summary II

In closing out this chapter let me say that the greatest danger concerning the sins of swearing and gossip is that many think that these are just minor sins, small vices that everyone does and thus not that serious. However, James says of the tongue and its sins:

> [5]So also the tongue is a small part of the body, and yet it boasts of great things. See how great a forest is set aflame by such a small fire! [6]And the tongue is a fire, the very world of iniquity; the tongue is set among our members as that which defiles the entire body, and sets on fire the course of our life, and is set on fire by hell.
> - James 3:5-6

I point this out for those who have problems in these areas so you will take seriously the lesson about these sins, and make a genuine effort to eliminate them from your lives because the reward (peace) is so great, and the punishment for these (hell) is so awful.

#7

PRIDE

In the Bible there are several root words in both the Hebrew and Greek language that are translated into the English words pride or proud. These Hebrew or Greek words in various forms also combine to give us other words which are similar to pride: haughty, vain, boastful, arrogant, disdainful, high-minded, etc.

There are many words used to describe the different shapes and manifestations of pride, but whatever the words they always go back to the source attitude which is pride.

The Hebrew and Greek words translated into English as the words pride or haughtiness are quite descriptive of this particular sin. For example, in the Old Testament the Hebrew words for pride meant:

- To mount up or to rise
- To be insolent
- To swell or to be high up
- To appear above
- To ascend
- To aspire to majesty

- Haughtiness
- To presume

In the New Testament the Greek words used to describe pride meant the following:

- To inflate
- To boast or brag
- To consume without fire (smoke)

All of these words were used to describe the sin of pride. The words give us a picture or idea of what pride is but not necessarily how it is a sin. Basically, the sin of pride occurs when we, in some way, leave or refuse to occupy our proper place in God's design.

Pride is usually exhibited in three ways:

1. When we improperly estimate our worth.

> For through the grace given to me I say to everyone among you not to think more highly of himself than he ought to think; but to think so as to have sound judgment, as God has allotted to each a measure of faith.
> - Romans 12:3

We often read or hear about people who have low self-esteem and the many problems that this personal condition causes. Pride is the opposite problem; a proud person has too high an esteem of himself or herself. This heightened self-esteem is exhibited in a variety of ways:

Arrogance – Thinking one's rights are primary over others. The complete disregard for other people's feelings or rights.

Boasting – Setting forth one's own talents, possessions and actions as superior because they are one's own.

Self-Righteousness – Assuming that our conduct, our ideas or lifestyle are better because they stem from ourselves.

Haughtiness – To assume that we are essentially more valuable because of the "position" we hold in society (i.e. royalty or movie stars).

There are other negative expressions of pride like condescension or self-centeredness, but you get the idea. Pride expresses itself, first of all, as an inordinately high estimate of our true worth as human beings.

2. When we measure our worth by the things we possess.

John calls this "…the boastful pride of life…" in I John 2:16. Whether it is a house, a car, an education, a name or a group we belong to, we feel superior because of what we possess. Another word for this type of pride is "status" or "class."

Much of the advertising on television or online appeals to this desire within people. The approach is, "If you own this (car, TV, jeans, make-up, etc.) you will be special, unique, better, smarter or cooler than those who do not possess these items." This is why some people will pay an extra 30% for a product with a particular emblem on it. This is pride by identification, vicarious pride or pride by exclusivity. We assume a "special" status by associating with someone famous or owning something that makes us better somehow than those who do not possess these things.

3. Pride as "self-sufficiency"

This type of pride exists in those who feel or believe that they are sufficient unto themselves. These are the people who believe that they, and they alone, control their own lives, and that whatever they have or have achieved is the result of their own efforts. They describe themselves as "self-made" people. They take great pride in their accomplishments and agonize over their defeats. These are the ones Paul refers to in Romans 1:22 when he says, "…professing to be wise."

This type of pride begins with self as the center of the universe and measures all else in the context of how it will positively or negatively affect self and one's sufficiency.

There may be other types of proud behavior but they can easily be fitted into one of these three categories: exaggerated self-worth, elevated status derived from things, and the desire to be totally "self-sufficient."

The Sin of Pride

Now that we have briefly described the sin of pride and how it is generally manifested, let us see why this attitude is considered sinful.

1. Exaggerated sense of worth

When we exaggerate our true value we are guilty of lying about ourselves. Pride, in this sense, is a delusion about self and who we really are. This false sense of self begins in our hearts.

[21] For from within, out of the heart of men, proceed

> the evil thoughts, fornications, thefts, murders, adulteries, [22] deeds of coveting and wickedness, as well as deceit, sensuality, envy, slander, pride and foolishness.
> - Mark 7:21-22

Isaiah explains that the root of pride is the desire to leave our place beneath the sovereignty of God and rise to a new and higher place, even putting ourselves above Him (Isaiah 14:12-16). Paul says that this sin is so pervasive that it infiltrates everyone's heart to some degree or another (II Corinthians 12:7).

It is the evil thought that somehow we are better than what God sees us as; or for those who don't believe in God, better because of the value we place on ourselves. It is this thought within our hearts that drives the arrogance, boasting, self-righteousness and haughtiness.

2. Pride in possessions

When it comes to pride based on the value of our possessions, the sin here is idolatry. When we draw our value and personal worth from the things we own, we are giving to these "things" the credit for who we are. This is a form of worship. If a person does this, he is investing his hope for self worth and value in something else other than God. The worship of an idol is not only confined to bowing down before a statue or image, it includes making gods out of the things we acquire or pursue by thinking they can make us better or happy.

The psalmist said in Psalm 52:7:

Behold, the man who would not make God his refuge, but trusted in the abundance of his riches and was strong in his evil desire.

We can derive satisfaction from our accomplishments and possessions, this is normal, but when "things" become the reason why we think we are better than others, then our pride has given these things an evil life of their own.

3. Pride in self-sufficiency

Self-sufficiency is the type of pride that is most condemned in the Bible because the sin inherent in this type of attitude is that of denying God and His power over us. Exaggerating our worth, or elevating our worth through things, these are sins that are committed with the knowledge of God. Self-sufficiency, however, says that, "I don't need God," or "There is no God, there is only me. As far as my world is concerned, I am God!" This dangerous sin is condemned vigorously throughout the Scriptures. For example:

> Therefore men fear Him; He does not regard any who are wise of heart.
> - Job 37:24

> The wicked, in the haughtiness of his countenance, does not seek Him. All his thoughts are, "There is no God."
> - Psalm 10:4

> There are six things which the Lord hates, yes, seven which are an abomination to Him: haughty eyes, a lying tongue, and hands that shed innocent blood.
> - Proverbs 6:16-17

> There is a kind who is pure in his own eyes, Yet is not washed from his filthiness.
> - Proverbs 30:12

> Therefore let him who thinks he stands take heed that he does not fall.
> - I Corinthians 10:12
>
> If we say that we have no sin, we are deceiving ourselves and the truth is not in us.
> - I John 1:8

To think that our position, talent, health or our very existence are somehow achieved apart from God is sinful, disrespectful and ingratitude. To think that goodness is sufficient to stand before God is both spiritual ignorance and boldness. To think that we don't need God every moment for everything is the height of spiritual blindness from which few ever recover. This is why the sin of pride is so dangerous.

Dealing with Pride

So far I have described the sin of pride in it's various expressions. I have also examined how and why these forms of pride are sinful, contrary to God's will and therefore wrong. Let us finish this chapter on pride with some teaching about how to deal with this very common sin in our lives.

1. Pride as an exaggerated sense of worth.

Many times when we do things or say things to raise ourselves up it comes from an incorrect view of our true worth. Solomon says that it is foolish to brag to others about ourselves because they often see the discrepancy between what we are and what we say we are (Proverbs 25:27). It is better, he says, to let another praise us since this will be a more legitimate assessment of our worth (Proverbs 27:2). In another proverb (11:2) he says that pride, contrary to our opinion, brings dishonor and not honor to the person.

In Romans 12:3 Paul tells Christians not to think of themselves more highly than they ought to. In other words, we should have an estimate of ourselves but it should be in line with reality. We should think no more or no less than what we really are.

In II Corinthians 10:18 Paul truly gets this issue of self-worth into perspective when he says:

For it is not he who commends himself that is approved, but he whom the Lord commends.

In other words, if the Lord approves of you, you are as worthy and valuable as anyone can ever become. As a matter of fact, for the Christian the only legitimate boasting is to boast about what Christ has accomplished in you. As Paul says:

> Most gladly, therefore, I will rather boast about my weaknesses, so that the power of Christ may dwell in me.
> - II Corinthians 12:9b

So if boasting/bragging is the form of pride you struggle with, remember that others are never impressed by it; and that the only legitimate boast is how much Christ has done through you.

2. Pride of life/possessions

In our nation this is the form of pride that most affects us. We live in a very materialistic society where the pressure to judge and value others by what they wear, drive, live is very powerful. We cannot leave this society and go live in a cave or a monastery. Jesus said that we lived *in* the world but must not be *of* the world. How, then, do we do this?

We do it by keeping our priorities in order. This is why Jesus said in Matthew 6:33, "Seek first His kingdom and His righteousness, and all these things will be added to you." This order requires you to seek first the things that are spiritual in nature; this would include God's will, God's work and God's purpose for your life. When these are the first priority God promises to provide (in His own way) the things you need. In other words, do not work for things, pray for things or be anxious for things. Instead, work for Him, pray for the knowledge of His will, be anxious to do what is right, and He will provide the things you need.

3. Pride – Self-Sufficiency

Finally, how do we overcome this most dangerous form of pride? The first step is recognizing that this is an area of concern in your life. Actually, the fact that you actually see it is a great sign of hope. Like all sins, to acknowledge it is the first and greatest step. I believe there are two ways God deals with those who struggle to resist becoming self-sufficient.

A. He warns them – For example in Psalm 49:11 it says, "For he sees that even the wise (self-sufficient) men die." And in Matthew 23:12 it reads, "And whoever exalts himself shall be humbled and whoever humbles himself shall be exalted." Through His word and His people God warns of the danger of this as well as every other sin. Some hear the warning and repent, others ignore it to their own destruction.

B. He disciples them – Sometimes God breaks a person down through trials and sorrows so that person will learn to lean on God. For example Nebuchadnezzar, the Babylonian King, went mad for several years before he regained his sanity and acknowledged God.

Another example of this is Paul the Apostle who was given a physical limitation so he would more closely depend on God.

In the end, what God wants is for us to completely rely on His word, His provision, His timing, His mercy, His Son and His church in order to become whole and pleasing in His sight. We lose our self-sufficient streak of pride when we are often in His word, often in prayer, patient for His will to be done, kind and generous toward others before self, following His Son and serving His church. When this is our lifestyle we have learned to die to self and live for Christ, and pride will no longer be our master.

#6

NEGLECTING CHURCH

We continue with our survey results of the top ten sins and struggles by looking at the problem of church neglect which came in at #6. This is a common problem so we will review the excuses most often given by those who do this and why it is important to make an effort to regularly attend all church services on Sunday and throughout the week.

Actually, people listed a variety of failings in this area of spiritual life:

- Neglecting attending church services
- Neglecting to give regularly
- Neglecting to serve in some way

Most struggles in one's spiritual life begin with or result in the habit of neglecting church services on a regular basis. Note that the Hebrew writer says,

> Let us consider how to stimulate one another to love and good deeds, not forsaking our own assembling together, as is the habit of some
> - Hebrews 10:25

In speaking of worship and other gatherings of the church, the writer encourages believers not to exchange the "habit" of coming to church for the habit of not coming to church. Therein lies the answer to the problem of neglecting worship and the other problems that stem from this (not giving or serving). If one can cultivate the habit of coming to church regularly, then the habits of giving and serving will follow suit.

Of course, regular church attendance has always been a problem (i.e. the letter to the Hebrews written in the first century admonishes the brethren about this very issue) and the excuses for neglect have always been the same. To help us become more faithful in this area I have compiled a list of the ten most common excuses for not coming to church that I have repeatedly heard in 38 years of full-time ministry, as well as three very good reasons for regular attendance so that taken together these can motivate Christians to be present at every service.

Top 10 Reasons for Missing Church

10. I am Jewish

Obviously the main reason why people do not come to church is because the vast majority of people in the world are not Christians. The number of believers in the world today is about the same as it was in 1830, but the world's population has gone from two billion at that time to over six billion today. This is why the great commission is still in force: more souls, but less Christians to bring the gospel to them. We need every Christian in church because every Christian is needed to carry out the great commission (Matthew 28:18-20).

9. I am Sick

Each week someone, among those who regularly attend, is ill or taking care of someone who is. This is normal. Church surveys tell us that five to ten percent of the members in any given congregation are dealing with illness that prevents them from attending. The danger here is that a period of illness often breaks the cycle of regular attendance and as result a formerly faithful member picks up the habit of irregular attendance. We need to watch out for that.

8. I am Changing

Life is a continual process of change (moving, college, marriage, babies, new jobs, more babies, etc.). With these changes come interruptions in our routines and habits. One habit that often suffers during a period of change is church attendance, just like it does when illness strikes. Coming to church sometimes gets packed away with other items that we promise to "sort out" once we get settled. Unfortunately, church attendance is one of those things that gets "unpacked."

7. I am Working

There was a time when industry and government recognized that this was a Christian country and working on Sundays or irregular shifts was less prevalent. Today our nation has become secularized where people accommodate worldly schedules, not the other way around. Providing for family is a priority (I Timothy 5:8). It is unfortunate, however, that society makes earning a living something that interferes more and more with our spiritual lives. Sometimes, I suspect, we work because we would rather get ahead in the world than get ahead in the kingdom.

6. I am New

One of the most embarrassing moments for the preacher is announcing the good news that we have a new brother or sister in Christ who has recently been baptized and ask them to stand at Sunday AM service only to find that they are not present. Later on we learn that they have not come for Wednesday services either. Young Christians may know about the gospel and how to be saved, but they also need to be trained in Christian living and patiently taught about the need and rewards of regular attendance. Their faith is weak and needs to be strengthened. Coming to church regularly is an acquired habit developed by word and example, but it has to be taught since it does not come automatically with baptism.

5. I am Busy

There is a difference between "I am working" and "I am busy"; one is need and the other is want. The busy person is not a bad person, just a busy person. In Mark 4:18-19 (The Sower and the Seed), Jesus describes this person as one who is concerned with problems, busy getting ahead, busy building a place for himself in this world, and as a consequence develops a priority problem. He/she allows the urgent things in this life to take over the important things. Busy people do not realize that God has promised that if we put kingdom things first (like church attendance) He will find a way to provide us with all those other things we are so busy trying to acquire for ourselves. The founder of the once popular department store chain, J.C. Penny, underscored this idea for his employees when he said, "If you are too busy to worship... you are too busy." This same sentiment is company policy for Chick-Fil-A, one of America's foremost fast food restaurants, as it embodies this spirit of correct priorities by closing all of its franchises on Sunday to allow its employees important family time.

A person who deliberately makes the time to worship God regularly offers to Him something valuable: his time, and this renders his worship pleasing and acceptable to God. The psalmist and great king, David, said,

> I refuse to offer God that which has cost me nothing.
> - II Samuel 24:24

4. I am Hurt

Many people come less and less to church because they have genuinely been hurt. Hurt by another member's comment, hurt by a perceived lack of attention by the leaders and ministers, hurt by some things that are being done in a way they do not agree with or hurt by a teacher's point of view on a particular Bible topic. It is unfortunate when this happens and I am persuaded that when there is an offense, it is never intentional. It is sad when people leave the church under such conditions, and unfortunate for two reasons:

1. Leaving the church because you are offended will not justify you before God. Jesus warned His disciples that they would be subjected to persecutions, false teachers and sufferings of all kinds (including hurt feelings). But He says, *"the one who endures to the end, he shall be saved."* (Mark 13:9-23) Regardless of the offense, leaving the church is rarely the answer nor is it something God excuses.

2. Stopping regular attendance because we are hurt or hurting (sometimes we are hurting because of some loss, tragedy or disappointment and we decide to take it out on God by ignoring Him) is never the answer. Jesus teaches us what we need to do when we are offended (go to the brother/sister in private, etc., Matthew 18:15), or hurting (ask for prayers and help, James 5:13). Let us not offend God for the offenses committed against us. Better that we "turn the other cheek" rather than abandon the one who died for us. That is why we offer an invitation at the end of every service, so we can minister to each other. Humbling ourselves and asking one another for help and prayer

in times of conflict or hurt builds trust and develops spiritual character.

3. I am Lazy

I have only met one person who actually sincerely acknowledged that this was the cause of many of his problems and failures, and I admire that person for their honesty. Let us face it, going to church on a regular basis requires physical and mental effort. There is preparation and travel (multiplied if you have kids, I feel for those moms who get those kids to church), discipline to sit and listen, and additional work involved if you are teaching, preaching or serving somehow. Then there is the mental effort required to take in information, and the spiritual effort necessary to make the continual adjustments and changes demanded by the Holy Spirit as He molds a Christ-like image in us.

The definition of a lazy person according to the dictionary is, "one who dislikes physical or mental effort." Proverbs says it in this way, *"The sluggard buries his hand in the dish; he is weary of bringing it to his mouth again."* (Proverbs 26:15) In other words, a lazy man will not even feed himself! The Lord provides for the nourishment of the only thing that will survive this world, a person's soul, and yet laziness keeps so many from feeding themselves on a regular basis. The best way to deal with laziness is to acknowledge it as a sin and ask God's help to overcome its many forms every day, especially on Sunday.

2. I am Worldly

One of the saddest stories in the Bible is the reference to Demas. In Colossians 4:14 and Philemon 24, Demas is counted among Paul's helpers and faithful disciples of the Lord. In his last letter from Rome, however, Paul refers to Demas, but this time he says, *"..for Demas, having loved this present world, has deserted me and gone to*

Thessalonica." (II Timothy 4:10) Some Christians do not attend church regularly because, like Demas, they love the world more than they love Christ. They love the smell of money more than the smell of the sacrifice of praise. They love the activity, the allurements and the pleasures of this world more than the activities, pleasures and promises of the next.

> This is the judgment, that the Light has come into the world, and men loved the darkness rather than the Light, for their deeds were evil.
> - John 3:19

When we are involved in a sin of some kind (i.e. a secret life) and have no desire to let it go or make no effort to struggle against it, we then lose interest in the light of truth shining upon us as it does when we worship God and study His word. Worldliness is such an insidious vice because it eats away at our spiritual life quietly and without pain until we are cold and dead in Christ but do not realize it until it is too late. We continually make one little concession to the world after another until we are no longer of the kingdom but of the world. This becomes evident because the first casualty of worldliness is our regular church attendance. Satan's number one strategy of attack is to diminish our exposure to God's word and other Christians, and he does this by finding all kinds of (reasonable) excuses for us to avoid regular church attendance.

1. I am _____

The number one reason, of course, is your reason for not being faithful to all the services of the church, whatever that may be. It could be any of the above or one I have not mentioned yet, but it is the number one reason if it keeps you out of church. For example, maybe you do not think you need to be at every service, maybe you are not convinced that the

Lord really wants this, perhaps you've abandoned the church because you feel that you are not getting anything out of church services. Whatever the reason, Satan has managed to find an opening in your spiritual defenses and has somehow convinced you that not attending all services is acceptable to God.

So much for excuses. There may be more but these ten probably include some that most Christians have used in one way or another to justify their absence from church services. In the last section of this chapter I'd like to look at some positive reasons why we should eagerly and joyfully attend every service of the church.

Reasons to Attend Regularly

Now some people ask, "Do I have to be there Sunday and Wednesday?" If you ask this question your problem is not attendance, your problem is love, gratitude and respect for God. We will deal with that later, for now, here are three reasons to come regularly:

1. Attending Every Time Pleases God

> [30]I will praise the name of God with song
> And magnify Him with thanksgiving.
> [31]And it will please the Lord better than an ox
> Or a young bull with horns and hoofs.
> - Psalms 69:30-31

God has always desired that His people gather to worship Him and that they do so often.

> [6]"Also the foreigners who join themselves to the
> Lord,

To minister to Him, and to love the name of the Lord,
To be His servants, every one who keeps from
profaning the sabbath
And holds fast My covenant;
[7]Even those I will bring to My holy mountain
And make them joyful in My house of prayer.
Their burnt offerings and their sacrifices will be
acceptable on My altar;
For My house will be called a house of prayer for all
the peoples."
- Isaiah 56:6-7

God was very specific about keeping the people true to the
day of worship and pleased with those who kept it.

[17]So then do not be foolish, but understand what the
will of the Lord is. [18]And do not get drunk with wine,
for that is dissipation, but be filled with the
Spirit, [19]speaking to one another in psalms and
hymns and spiritual songs, singing and making
melody with your heart to the Lord;
- Ephesians 5:17-19

God desires that we be involved in this type of activity when
we are together rather than chase worldly pursuits. You have
a choice of activity on Sundays and Wednesdays. Worship
will always be the thing that pleases God.

[15]Through Him then, let us continually offer up a
sacrifice of praise to God, that is, the fruit of lips that
give thanks to His name. [16]And do not neglect doing
good and sharing, for with such sacrifices God is
pleased.
- Hebrews 13:15-16

God is pleased to see us offering Him praise. God is the same in the Old and New Testaments.

Pleasing God is what our lives are about, to know and glorify Him is the essential meaning of life. When we worship Him we know we are doing the right thing. When we worship, we have reached the zenith of what life is all about. Not coming requires an excuse (good or bad), but being present at worship never requires an excuse. Our conscience is clear because we are doing the absolute right thing. Most people want to please those that they love, this is a plain truth. Being present at every worship service pleases God and demonstrates our love for Him.

Unfortunately, our sinful flesh would rather please ourselves and make church attendance convenient, fun, easy, pleasant, etc., but we need to remember that the object of our worship is to please God, not ourselves!

2. Being at Every Service Strengthens Your Faith

When people have problems and you ask them what they need, aside from physical help, they usually ask for more faith. The Apostles witnessed the miracles of Jesus and yet when it came time to ask Him for something, they asked Him to increase their faith (Luke 17:5). Faith is not only necessary for salvation but is also necessary to be able to persevere through the ups and downs of life so we can maintain that salvation.

Faith is such an important thing, but how do you acquire it and how do you strengthen it?

> So faith comes from hearing, and hearing by the word of Christ.
> - Romans 10:17

All the activities in the world combined do not add a single measure to our faith. Hearing, sharing and learning God's word, this sparks faith and helps it to grow.

What you are able to do in the name of the Lord (i.e. resist sin, persevere in suffering, doing good, bearing spiritual fruit, etc.) is all based on the strength of your faith, and the strength of your faith is proportional to your exposure to God's word and God's people. There are no short-cuts. Weak attendance equals weak Christians with weak faith who produce little spiritual fruit. Strong faith is usually a result of much teaching, and for most Christians that only comes through regular attendance.

Some will inevitably ask, "If I only come to Sunday AM worship and skip the rest, can I still go to heaven?" My personal answer to this is: probably not, not because you do not come regularly but because your question tells me that you are a legalist doing only what you have to do. You have fallen from grace and are trying to justify yourself with religious works, and minimum religious works at that! This question shows a lack of knowledge regarding the faith. You need to come to church, not to increase your attendance level, you need to come to church so you can learn about God's grace and be free from the Law. If you keep this attitude, no amount of church attendance will save you. I am not saying, "If you do not go to Wednesday night Bible study, you are going to hell." I am saying that if this is your attitude you are a legalist and fallen from grace. We are saved by faith: we see by faith, we walk by faith, we can cast mountains into the ocean by faith, and that faith is conceived and nourished every time we attend church services. Why come to church every time? Because every time we leave, we leave with a stronger faith.

3. Your Attendance Builds the Church

> [23]Let us hold fast the confession of our hope without wavering, for He who promised is faithful; [24]and let us consider how to stimulate one another to love and good deeds, [25]not forsaking our own assembling together, as is the habit of some, but encouraging one another; and all the more as you see the day drawing near.
> - Hebrews 10:23-25

The problem that these Jewish Christians struggled with was that they were weak in the faith and were being tempted to return to Judaism as a consequence of their spiritual immaturity. Their absence from the assembly contributed to their weak faith and their weak faith could not sustain them when under pressure. In addition to this, their absence was hurting others. This is why the writer of this letter encourages them not to abandon the assembly and exhorts them to give an example and word of encouragement to others about this as well.

Presence at all services is critical in the building up of the church. Through regular attendance at all services:

1. We proclaim Christ to each other and the community (I Corinthians 11:26).

2. We provide an example to others (Hebrews 10:23-29). What do you think our absence says to children and younger Christians? It says, "When I grow up or when I am an experienced saint it will be acceptable to skip church." Unfortunately, it is not acceptable and a member's absence without cause harms the church.

3. By attending all services we contribute towards the needs of the saints (I Corinthians 16:1-7). Not just by

giving money, but by knowing who needs help and learning how we can serve.

4. We demonstrate our support for the leadership of the church. The elders have set these worship times as a way of protecting and feeding our souls. Refusing to come is a refusal of this leadership. The Bible says we must submit to those whom the Lord has set over us in Christ (Hebrews 13:17).

We build the place where the saints meet for worship with wood and brick, but faithfulness to all the services is the cornerstone upon which the building of the congregation itself rests.

Summary

As I close I want to say to all those who listed "church attendance" as a problem that their struggle is nothing new. It was there when He church was established (Hebrews 10:25) and the Bible says it will be there until the end of the world (Matthew 24:12). The solution then, now and in the future, has always been and will always be the same:

1. Begin to cultivate the habit of regular attendance to all services.

2. Get involved in the work of the church.

3. Realize that coming to church is always the best choice and God will reward you for it.

#5

COPING WITH CHANGE

A common areas where Christians struggle is the power of "changing circumstances" to affect their faith and Christian practice in a negative way. For example:

- Your elderly mother is put into a nursing facility, leaving your dad alone at home.

- You live 120 miles away; your younger, unmarried brother lives in the same town.

Can you see the "problems" that will arise with these changes in living arrangements?

- Conflict as to who is primary care giver.

- Loss of work and family time traveling back and forth.

- Decision whether to bring dad in with kids or nursing home with mom.

- Broken routine of regular worship.

- Conflict over financial responsibility for care expenses, etc.

For example the following situation:

- You've just moved to a new city with your family.

- You're happy for a new job, new opportunity.

- Your wife misses her parents and your children are having trouble in their new school.

- The church you now go to has less people and programs than your old one.

- What will be some of the issues here?

    o More arguments.

    o Stress for failure of children in school.

    o Loss of intimacy because of pressure and anxiety.

I give two common types of experiences to show that "changes" bring new situations to get used to and new problems to solve. These bring stress, anxiety, depression, even physical illness or family breakdown.

So whether it's:

- A new school

- Declining health (yours or family member)

- Moving

- A first or subsequent marriage or the breakup of a marriage

- A new baby or job or retirement from a job

- A failure of some kind of adapting to greater responsibility

Changes are difficult and learning to cope with change is a large part of our maturing process - older you get the more changes there are. Now changes in every area of our lives are inevitable, there will always be changes, we cannot avoid the fact that our lives will encounter change from time to time (some for good, others not so good).

So the first thing we need to understand and accept is that there will be change, no need to be surprised or upset when it finally occurs.

If we accept that change is a natural (if not always easy) part of life, we can more easily learn the things we need to do to cope with it.

Coping with Change

Obviously this lesson will not exhaust all of the more positive ways to deal/cope successfully with change.

Hopefully, what I share with you will help you see what God provides us with in order to support us in times of change in our lives.

1. Keep "Change" in Perspective

There is an ebb and flow to life that bring natural changes with them - try to keep this in mind. Solomon said that there was a "time" for everything under the sun and all the things he mentions in Ecc. 3 have to do with change

Birth, death, beginnings and endings, war and peace, searching, giving up, building and tearing down...are not all these things part of change?

The "coping" problem that change engenders is one of dealing with how we feel about the different set of circumstances that face us due to change. We get nervous and depressed because we think:

- The change will change everything, when in reality only a part of our lives will be different.

- The change is too fast, when the real problem is that we're slow in accepting the inevitable.

- The change is for the worse, we say this because we are judging only the immediate results and not the long term effects that may yield good fruit.

- The change is not what you wanted, of course we think this when our will is crossed, but since when is our will the criteria for what is good or best?

Change is less unsettling when we can see the big picture and not just the small universe of our own lives.

For example:

- Children marrying (even marrying someone we're not crazy about) may be traumatic for the moment, but in the long run many children realize that they want peace with mom and dad, and they want their parents' support as they begin raising their own families.

- It was difficult for some of our members here when we went to bilingual services because each group (Eng/Fr) lost some intimacy and convenience of always speaking their own language. But look at what we gained in rich fellowship and a more satisfying worship all together.

Keeping "change" in the perspective that:

- Changes in life are constant and

- Most changes work out in the long run.

Keeping this perspective helps lower the panic and fear level that comes along with the many changes we face in life. Another way to cope with change more successfully is to…

2. Entrust God with the Changes

One of the questions that most epitomizes how we feel about change is the following: "How will I ever be able to deal with this change?" All this talk about the difficulty of dealing or coping with change is usually a sign of fear:

- Fear that we won't be able to adjust.

- Fear that we'll be left behind.

- Fear that the pain will be too great.

- Fear that what was precious or comfortable for us will be lost forever.

- Fear we won't like what change brings.

Now I'm not saying that these are not legitimate feelings and concerns.

- A woman has surgery for breast cancer and her concern for the changes that will result from this is real.

- A 47 year old man loses his job with the company he's worked for for 25 years and this will bring serious change into his life.

- A couple decides to sell their home and move to a retirement community.

- A young person chooses to go to college far away from home.

- A young couple has their first baby.

These are real life scenarios that will cause upheaval and uncertainty in anyone who experiences these kinds of changes in their lives.

Of course there will be fear, anxiety and stress, but what I'm saying is that there doesn't only have to be fear, anxiety and stress. For the Christian there is the avenue of prayer that brings us into the presence and protection of almighty God.

In Hebrews 13, the writer expresses his utmost trust in God in the face of all circumstances when he writes:

> "Let your character be free from the love of money, being content with what you have; for He Himself has said, 'I will never desert you nor will I forsake you,' so that we confidently say - 'The Lord is my helper, I will not be afraid. What shall man do unto me?'"
> - Hebrews 13:5-6.

Of course change is threatening, frightening and difficult - but it is not impossible, nor does it have to be the cause for a negative experience. God assures us that He will always be with us to watch over us and to provide.

It's easy to believe this while times are stable and predictable. It's when we find ourselves in the eye of the storm that this promise is difficult to believe. But this of it, is anything too difficult for God? Do changes confuse God or make it any more difficult for Him to care for us?

On the contrary, I have found that it is in the process of change and upheaval that my relationship with God grows stronger, more intimate and more spiritually satisfying.

Perhaps this is because while everything around me seems to constantly be changing, I then see more clearly the unchanging nature of God's love and care for me that remains solid as a rock.

Summary

Different people react to "change" in different ways:

A. Resignation

Some simply resign themselves to it. This is a kind of a passive/aggressive approach to change. They don't resist it but they don't accept it either. The change doesn't change them, it merely changes their circumstances.

B. Resistance

Some fight change - any kind of change. This is how they cope with it, they resist it. Sometimes we do have to resist change because the change is a bad one. But some people resist change because they are against any change at all.

C. Repetition

And still others promote change. These people love change because change is the antidote to their boredom and lack of sense of self. These are the folks who make change happen because they like change - any change.

Hopefully I have described to you a more healthy and Biblical approach to dealing with change in your lives:

- **Accept the fact that changes in life are natural and inevitable.** Don't be surprised or hurt or panicked because change is normal.

- **Try to keep the changes in your life in proper perspective.** Don't overreact or overestimate the impact of changes you face.

- **Put your trust in God.** God is aware of every change and circumstance, we need to trust Him with the outcome of the changes in our lives.

Whatever we need, He will provide, whatever we lose, He will restore in His own way. Of course there is one final change we all should look forward to as Christians and that is the change we will undergo when Jesus returns. Our mortal bodies will be transformed (changed) into glorious ones in order to dwell in heaven with God forever (I Thessalonians 4:17 - no more change).

So in a way, the many changes we undergo in life prepare us to experience the greatest and final change when Jesus comes. Let's cope with change with faith, trust and hope that we will be found worthy to be changed into glory when the time comes.

#5

COPING WITH CONFLICT

It is no wonder that conflict issues are on the list because conflict is all we read about and see in the news and witness all around us. Whether it is conflict between nations, races or political factions, or the day to day conflicts we experience at home, work or school, all conflict has an effect on us.

We've seen examples, we know conflict when we see it, but can we define it?

The dictionary defines conflict as:

- A struggle between opposing principles or aims.
- A clash of feelings or interests.

Isn't it interesting that the #10 sin or struggle named in our survey was "struggle" itself? The definition in the dictionary sheds light on the cause of most conflicts whether they be countries, or partners in a marriage, or two people working in the same office.

In its simplest form we can say that conflict is caused by how we react or handle differences. If we lived alone on islands there might be struggle to survive in finding food and shelter, but there would be no conflict because everything would be done "our way." But we don't live on islands and our way of thinking or doing things bumps up against other people in our homes, family, community and the world at large who think and do things "their way."

Now when our way and their way are similar in approach and objective there is harmony, however when their way and our way are very different or have different goals the possibility for conflict arises. Of course, it's not just that their way and our way are different, there are other factors that contribute to conflict:

1. Perception

The problem between our way and their way is often one of perception. We do not always perceive things in the way they really are. This happens because we do not take the time to listen properly or we do not make an effort to understand. Sometimes we have been given wrong information so our opinion has been prejudiced. In cases like these we react negatively to "their way" because we perceive their way to be:

- Not good, weak, not true, etc.
- Dangerous
- Against our way somehow
- Not able to achieve the goal

In the end, if our perception of their way is negative (for whatever reason) we will enter into a conflict to replace their way with our way.

2. Pride

We think "our way" in whatever context is always the "best way." So long as everyone else goes along with our way there is no conflict. There are many reasons for this type of attitude, but the most common one is having a false estimate of our true worth. Some people suffer from low self-esteem and falsely think they are not worthy; others suffer from an overly high esteem of themselves and believe that they are more than worthy. It is this type of attitude that often leads to conflict with others.

Pride over culture leads to war and mass murder. Pride for "our way" destroys couples in marriage, partners in business, friends at school and brethren in the church.

When we assume that our way is best we will always be in conflict, it will be the defining experience of our lives.

3. Politics

When I say politics I am not referring to government or political parties. Politics is the word used to refer to the games people play in order to get "their way." Governments play politics so they can hold on to power in order to exercise their way in running the country. I'm referring to strategies and methods that groups and individuals use in order to impose their will.

Some are brutal, like in many countries where the government uses force to impose their will on the people. Some are subtle, like a young child manipulating one parent against another in order to get a new toy.

Politics (the way we get our way) has an effect on the intensity of conflict we will experience. For example, government brutality often gives rise to resistance movements and civil wars as one group pushes back against another thus creating social conflict. A domineering boss who insists on her way without considering feedback from co-workers may unintensionally foster employees who become passive aggressive in their behavior in order to block her plans out of spite. The husband who thinks his opinion on everything is correct may create a wife who challenges him on every matter just to prove him wrong. The resulting situation in all of these scenarios is conflict.

And so the list goes on in the various ways conflict can arise based on how we impose "our way" over "their way." Our politics are formed by our ethics (our sense of what is right and wrong) and so how we impose our way will be guided by what we believe is right and wrong.

This is true for governments as well as married couples, people at work, family and friends. How and when we choose to get "our way" will play a large factor in how much conflict we experience.

The Bible and Conflict

Of course the subject of conflict is a very wide and complicated one, but not impossible. We can make some general observations as to the causes of conflict.

- Perception   - my way is better
- Pride   - my way is best
- Politics   - my way by any means.

In the same way, I think we can make some suggestions from the Bible as to how we can avoid or at least lower the frequency and intensity of the conflict in our lives.

1. Examine "our way"

Let's face it, the reason for most of the conflicts in our lives is that we are not able to get "our way" somehow.

> [1] What is the source of quarrels and conflicts among you? Is not the source your pleasures that wage war

> in your members? [2] You lust and do not have; so you
> commit murder. You are envious and cannot obtain;
> so you fight and quarrel. You do not have because
> you do not ask. [3] You ask and do not receive,
> because you ask with wrong motives, so that you
> may spend it on your pleasures.
> - James 4:1-3

When we don't get "our way" in our personal relationships, jobs, family, etc. we begin to examine the person or the situation blocking our way. Conflicts are rarely resolved without a change of some kind, but they persist because we always expect the change to come from someone else! We want them to change "their way" in order to accommodate "our way" because our way is right, better, more comfortable, or just - our way.

> For through the grace given to me I say to everyone
> among you not to think more highly of himself than
> he ought to think; but to think so as to have sound
> judgement, as God has allotted to each a measure of
> faith.
> - Romans 12:3

God tells us through Paul to be honest in how we are to evaluate ourselves (includes "our way"). Don't measure yourself by yourself, but rather by the faith God has given you. The "faith" is the body of teaching provided by God in His word. In other words, Christians don't have "their way" they have "God's way" of dealing with things dictated by His word.

Paul says to measure your way against His way in order to be sure that they are compatible. A person's estimate of himself is too high if he insists that his own way is better than God's way. This type of attitude smacks of pride and leads to conflict. Usually conflict is avoided or greatly reduced when we seek to follow God's way in our dealings with others. Examples of God's way replacing our way when in conflict situations include, but are certainly not limited to:

> A gentle answer deflects anger but harsh words make tempers flare.
> - Proverbs 15:1

Instead of, fight fire with fire.

> Love each other with genuine affection and take delight in honoring one another.
> - Romans 12:10

Instead of, my way or the highway.

We always need to be aware of what we are contributing to the conflict that we are experiencing:

- Is it our pride, misunderstanding, prejudice or approach that may be pouring gasoline on the fire?
- Am I dealing with their way using God's way or my way?
- How much of this conflict am I responsible for?

An honest (meaning a judgment based on God's word) estimate of ourselves is always the beginning of the end of conflict.

2. Expect conflict

There will always be conflict. As Christians we need to minimize what we do to create, intensify or prolong conflict, but we also need to be realistic and accept that we cannot eliminate all conflict. We've not been called by God to stop all conflict in the world; this isn't the purpose of Christianity.

Jesus said that there would always be conflict of some kind in the world.

> [4] And Jesus answered and said to them, "See to it that no one misleads you. [5] For many will come in My name, saying, 'I am the Christ,' and will mislead many. [6] You will be hearing of wars and rumors of wars. See that you are not frightened, for those things must take place, but that is not yet the end. [7] For nation will rise against nation, and kingdom against kingdom, and in various places there will be famines and earthquakes. [8]But all these things are merely the beginning of birth pangs.
> - Matthew 24:4-8

He even warned His disciples that because of their faith in Him they would be drawn into conflict.

> [34] Do not think that I came to bring peace on the earth; I did not come to bring peace, but a sword. [35] For I came to set a man against his father, and a daughter against her mother, and a daughter-in-law against her mother-in-law; [36] and a man's enemies will be the members of his household.
> - Matthew 10:34-36

The only conflict we engage in is the one that involves disbelief and belief in Jesus Christ. This conflict/struggle will always be present within ourselves as we strive to live by the Spirit and not by the flesh. In addition to this we will be constantly challenged to stand up for the faith in the presence of a disbelieving world.

There is always conflict of some kind, but Christians focus on the conflict involved in establishing the spiritual kingdom and try to minimize others. Obviously, conflict in the world is largely due to sin of some kind, and in the world there is great effort to resolve or win conflicts using a variety of man-made approaches such as force, social activism, diplomacy, mediation, etc.

As Christians we don't deny that these conflicts do and will continue to exist, and that these methods or resolutions work to a certain extent. However, we also believe that the ultimate solution to conflict whether it be between two countries or a mother and her daughter, is peace through faith and submission to Jesus Christ by both parties. This may seem foolish to the world, but it always succeeds when attempted.

We accept that there will always be conflict but we choose the conflict that we will engage in as Christians, and how we will fight.

[10] Finally, be strong in the Lord and in the strength of His might. [11] Put on the full armor of God, so that you will be able to stand firm against the schemes of the devil. [12] For our struggle is not against flesh and blood, but against the rulers, against the powers, against the world forces of this darkness, against the spiritual forces of wickedness in the heavenly places. [13] Therefore, take up the full armor of God, so that you will be able to resist in the evil day, and having done everything, to stand firm. [14] Stand firm therefore, having girded your loins with truth, and having put on the breastplate of righteousness,[15] and having shod your feet with the preparation of the gospel of peace; [16] in addition to all, taking up the shield of faith with which you will be able to extinguish all the flaming arrows of the evil one. [17] And take the helmet of salvation, and the sword of the Spirit, which is the word of God.
- Ephesians 6:10-17

3. Engage God in prayer

I know that going to God in prayer is a pretty standard answer for all of life's issues, but it is especially important in times of conflict. If there is ever a time for fervent prayer it is when we are in conflict. Usually the conflict is painful, or threatening, creating all kinds of upheaval and change in our lives. Many cannot sleep, think straight, lose their sense of humor, joy and ability to focus.

Many times conflict is simply a diversion by Satan to prepare us for a fall of some kind. For example:

- Cain was in conflict with Abel over the appropriateness of his sacrifice and his anger and resentment led him to kill his brother.

- Paul and Barnabas were in conflict over Mark's conduct during their first missionary journey and their conflict could have threatened the future of Paul's important mission work.

When we are in conflict we are vulnerable, so we must take extra care and time to lay our case, our thoughts, our frustrations and our pain before God in prayer. The goal is to see "His way" forward, His solution and His insight to guide us.

Many times when we are in conflict we will pray about the situation, but neglect to do the second and more difficult part of prayer which is waiting for an answer and waiting for God to act.

> Be still and know that I am God.
> - Psalm 46:10

The Word tells us that God will direct us, teach us and show us the right way.

> Show me the right path O Lord, point out the road for me to follow.
> - Psalm 25:4

When we are in conflict, too often we try to resolve it ourselves without waiting for God to guide our actions or act on our behalf. Whether it is a conflict with a friend, a conflict inwardly, a conflict in living the right way as a Christian, or conflicts with our spouse - engage the Lord in prayer and wait for His leading out of conflict.

God knows the root and solution to all conflicts in our lives. Prayer helps us to not only see what God sees, it also helps us to do what is necessary in order to reduce the conflict and have peace. This peace is not the peace that the world offers with truces and treaties - but the peace that can only come through Jesus Christ and surpasses human understanding.

Summary

We are in conflict with God and each other because of sin, and Jesus makes peace with God on our behalf through His death on the cross. Each of us can now have peace with God through the forgiveness of our sins when we believe in Christ, repent of our sins and are baptized in His name. Once we have this blessed peace with God we have the Spirit's power within us to be at peace with all men.

#4

EASILY DISCOURAGED

Before we go directly to the issue of easy discouragement, I'd like to comment on the reality of discouragement. There's this false idea that Christians are immune from being discouraged.

For example:

- Your house burns down and you have no insurance? Hallelujah, praise the Lord anyways!

- You've just been informed that you have cancer? Nothing to worry about, God won't put anything on me that I can't handle.

- Your Christian brother has lost his wife and is very depressed?Get in there and cheer him up, he'll see her in heaven some day.

There is this unhealthy and unbiblical push to deny the very real truth that sometimes life is very sad, very difficult, very very discouraging. Of course we want to hope for a better day, relief from our sorrows, a happy ending, but when these are slow in coming or don't come at all - it is natural to feel discouraged.

Some people actually feel guilty because they feel they ought never to feel discouraged as Christians. Solomon said there was a time for everything and that includes discouragement. Discouragement is a natural feeling caused by adversity.

The key is to not allow this feeling to lead you into a loss of faith or hope or love.

Being easily discouraged is different than simply being discouraged. Being discouraged is a feeling that comes with renewed failure, consistent adversity, repeated rejection and loss. Being easily discouraged is becoming negative and unsure at the first sign of trouble; it's giving up without even making an effort. These two sound the same but are really different problems and require different approaches to resolve.

1. Discouraged

Overcoming discouragement requires less the adjustment of our attitude and more the adjustment of our approach. It's natural to feel discouraged if we're rejected or fail at something or are burdened with too much:

- Work/deadlines
- Responsibilities
- Information
- Emotional stimulus

Feeling discouraged is our body's way of telling us we may be outmatched, outnumbered. Whatever is before us is more than we can handle (for some reason) and the discouragement we feel is our body's way of registering that fact.

Sometimes we have to go a long time before we feel this way. We've gone 8 or 9 rounds with the project, the illness, the relationship, the problem…before we start feeling discouraged. But when it comes, that feeling signals the fact that we may not be winning or succeeding regardless of our best efforts and strategies and prayers.

Here are three things to do when we are genuinely and rightfully discouraged by the situation we find ourselves in, or facing another round with a difficult opponent.

A. Re-Commit

In some situations such as marriage or leadership roles, where a deep commitment is made and necessary, some of our problem may be that we're getting shaky in our commitment and it's affecting our actions.

Christians, who have a lifetime commitment, often get discouraged along the way because they secretly begin to doubt and as a result their commitment wavers and so does their ability to follow the Way.

Do I believe or not; am I going to follow through or not; till death do us part or not?

Many times a re-commitment to our core values will send a shot of adrenalin through the entire system which will in turn enable us to succeed where we once failed, or give us the strength to accept the situation or failure we have encountered, in a positive and hopeful way.

B. Re-Examine

Only a fool will continue repeating the same methods when they repeatedly fail. When we're in the heat of battle we think, "If I just try a little harder, I'll win the day." So we exert more pressure, more energy, more will-power and still fail…and of course feel discouraged.

Hopefully, before we wear out and burn up all of our resources, discouragement will make us step back and look at ourselves rather than our problem. Many times the trouble is with us, the problem is our approach, solution, attitude.

This is a good time to ask for help, for a second opinion - Solomon said,

> Without consultation plans are frustrated, but with many counselors they succeed.
> - Proverbs 15:22.

C. Relax

Many times our discouragements are, as the great writer once said, "Much ado about nothing." We either overreact over small matters or get run over by a freight train of trouble we couldn't stop no matter how hard we tried.

Either way, we become emotionally exhausted and spiritually spent leading to that queasy feeling of discouragement. Our fatigue becomes our worse enemy because it makes us unable to deal with other issues leading to further discouragement and despair. We have to learn to relax (yes relaxing is a "learned" ability). Here are a few things you have to know in order to learn how to relax:

- Know when to take a break.

    - Unbroken effort leads to strain and loss of perspective.

    - Allow yourself a "time-out" from your problem, challenge, whatever so you can regain your perspective.

    - When I'm behind in my study or my lesson is just not coming together, I let it go and do something completely different for awhile before I come back to it.

- o Jesus often took His disciples away to a quiet spot so they could recharge.

- Know your limits.

  - o Every person has a "burn-out" point. It's different with each one.

  - o Discouragement is a yellow warning light that you're getting close to yours.

  - o Don't extend your limits, it will not help your discouragement nor will it solve your problems.

- Know who is in charge.

  - o Much discouragement is the result of human effort without reference to God's presence.

  - o We push and we try and we grit our teeth but the rock of our discouragement won't move.

  - o And yet Jesus said, "If you have faith as a mustard seed, you shall say to this mountain, 'Move from here to there' and it shall move. And nothing shall be impossible for you." Matthew 17:20

Relax and remember to take a break realizing that you are a weak human being and that in the end God's will must be done I your life. And so discouragements will come because there is always adversity in life, but when discouragement comes: re-commit to your basic core values and beliefs; re-examine yourself and be ready to try a new approach; learn to relax - God is still in charge, He will give you the victory or the courage to live with loss - all according to your faith and trust in Him.

2. Being Easily Discouraged

As I said before, being easily discouraged is a different problem than being discouraged. Discouragement is a natural byproduct of repeated failure or on-going problems. Easy discouragement has a different source and cause. People become easily discouraged because they lack:

A. Core values and beliefs greater than themselves.

You see, what enables a person to persevere despite discouragement is usually the fact that they hold to a belief or value system greater than themselves. People die for their country, their ideals, to protect their home and family, as a witness of their faith. When discouragement comes, they look to their beliefs and values to sustain them and comfort them and motivate them to press on.

In Matthew 13:1-23, Jesus explains this principle in light of the Christian faith using the parable of the Sower and the seed.

> [3] And He spoke many things to them in parables, saying, "Behold, the sower went out to sow; [4] and as he sowed, some seeds fell beside the road, and the birds came and ate them up. [5] Others fell on the rocky places, where they did not have much soil; and immediately they sprang up, because they had no depth of soil. [6] But when the sun had risen, they were scorched; and because they had no root, they withered away. [7] Others fell among the thorns, and the thorns came up and choked them out. [8] And others fell on the good soil and yielded a crop, some a hundredfold, some sixty, and some thirty. [9] He who

has ears, let him hear."
- Matthew 13:3-9

Note the seed on rocky places comes up fairly quickly, there's shallow dirt so the plant has to break through to survive, having no deep root system.

> [20] The one on whom seed was sown on the rocky places, this is the man who hears the word and immediately receives it with joy; [21] yet he has no firm root in himself, but is only temporary, and when affliction or persecution arises because of the word, immediately he falls away.
> - Matthew 13:20-21

Immediately falling away is "easily discouraged." Why? No firm root within. In gardening, if the plant has no extensive root system to find water in dry times - it will dry up and die. In human terms the "root system" is our core system of faith, a faith that has broken the surface of our hard, sinful hearts and established itself firmly within us.

People can do the easy stuff of religion like go to church, enjoy the fellowship, hear the good news of heaven, receive ministry.

But when the hard stuff comes along like...

- Resisting fleshly lusts
- Doing the right thing, even if it costs us
- Serving others despite the inconvenience
- Persevering through difficult trials

...someone whose faith is only skin deep, who doesn't base decisions on their convictions about Christ - this person will become easily discouraged.

Another reason for easy discouragement is:

B. Self Reliance

If you're often easily discouraged, one reason may be that you rely on yourself too much. The Psalmists said of the Israelites,

> "For by their own sword they did not possess the land and their own arm did not save them. But Thy right hand, and Thine arm, and the light of Thy presence, for Thou didst favor them."
> - Psalm 44:3

Self-reliance, self-made, self-sufficiency is man's greatest goal and his greatest delusion. The Psalmists put this concept into perspective when speaking of man's position in regards to God in the matter of supplying needs:

> "..For His loving kindness is everlasting who gives food to all flesh."
> - Psalm 136:25

> "..My flesh and my heart may fail, but God is the strength of my heart and my position forever."
> - Psalm 73:26

People who have only themselves to rely on, or rely only on human wisdom (doctors, lawyers, teachers, etc.) quickly lose heart when they realize how puny, how futile human wisdom and strength are. Oh, some may persevere for communism or laugh unrepentingly in the face of death caused by their AIDS - but they are simply more deluded than the rest. People who don't know God and His word are easily discouraged when their mask of self-reliance is quickly ripped off by a sudden calamity.

The final cause of easy discouragement is

C. Distraction

I go back to Jesus' parable of the sower and the seed.

> And the one on whom seed was sown among the thorns, this is the man who hears the word, and the worry of the world and the deceitfulness of wealth choke the word, and it becomes unfruitful.
> - Matthew 13:22

Notice that what cost this person his soul was not some great immorality or a lot of adversity - he was distracted. He allowed the normal things that clamor for attention to divert his attention from where it should be. The word "worry" or "cares" in some Bibles comes from a Greek word which means to separate, to divert, to distract. He allowed the riches of this world to give him the false impression that they were worthy of his attention.

The net result was that he became focused on the wrong things and consequently the word; the Sprit; the kingdom began to lose its influence and power in and over him. One of the fruits of the Spirit is perseverance. We are left to conclude that when adversity did come, he quickly became discouraged in Christ because he had lost his focus.

The danger of so much "busyness" in the world is that it leads us to distraction and distraction ultimately leads to discouragement.

Summary

1. Discouragement is normal. It's our emotional alarm that we are fighting a losing battle.

2. There are things to do in cases of legitimate discouragement. Re-examine your core beliefs and reasons for where you're at. Re-commit to valid promises. Relax, let go and let God.

3. Being easily discouraged is not normal. Often caused by lack of core values/beliefs, self reliance and distraction.

4. One main thing to do to overcome easy discouragement: focus and stay focused on God's word. It will instill a bed-rock faith in the Lord Jesus Christ as Lord and Savior - Romans 10:17. It will reveal God's eternal promises that will provide comfort and hope in every time of your life - Ephesians 1:3-14. It will help you remain focused and fruitful as you await the return of Jesus Christ - Matthew 13:23 (the seed sown in the lowest heart bearing fruit).

If this is your problem and you want to do something concrete to overcome - commit yourself to becoming a regular Bible reader and see how your life will begin to change because of it.

#3

OVERANXIOUS

Let us begin with our countdown of the top ten sins and struggles:

- #10: Laziness
- #9: Anger
- #8: Cursing and Gossip
- #7: Pride
- #6: Neglecting Church
- #5: Coping with Change
- #4: Easily Discouraged
- #3: Overanxious (Worry)

This is another "struggle" issue. Worry all by itself is not a problem of morality, although in one sense when we as Christians worry we are disobeying Jesus who said not to worry (Matthew 6:31). Of course, that this struggle was named by so many people is no surprise because it has always been a common and negative human reaction experienced by both believers and nonbelievers.

Let us, therefore, look at this issue and some of the remedies for it.

Overanxious (Worry)

What is worry? For most people worry is a feeling of fear or unhappiness regarding something or someone. It usually consists of negative speculation about something that may happen in the future (one minute or one year hence, but always in the future). We feel regret, shame or guilt for the past, but worry is always focused on something in the future. These include things like the condition of our health, the safety of our family and the need to provide for our needs. We worry about simple things like the look of our appearance or complex issues that involve marital disputes or the care of elderly parents.

There is, however, a difference between worry and concern. Unlike worry, which has a negative effect on us, concern or focused attention usually helps us avoid trouble and pain. The only tangible product of worry, on the other hand, is over-stress caused by the anxiety stirred up because of our constant worry. Worry saps us of energy, wastes time, is discouraging and robs us of the enthusiasm needed to succeed in our work, family life and service to the church. Some people invest so much of their energy into worry that they have precious little of it left to take care of the problems facing them today. God provides us with the emotional resources we need to deal with each day's challenges, but if we constantly waste these resources in worrying about tomorrow, today's problems will invariably overwhelm us and create a negative cycle leading to depression and burn-out.

We worry about tomorrow but do not know what tomorrow will bring. If we did, we could do something about it and change worry into action. But we do not and thus waste energy and time worrying, and create unneeded stress that leads to burn-out. Of course, we know all of this but continue to worry anyways because worry is the "go to" emotion we have cultivated through years of constant repetition. Is there anything to do to avoid this debilitating habit?

Jesus and James both teach valuable lessons concerning worry and how we can eliminate this negative emotional habit and replace it with things that actually help us reduce the stress caused by the challenges that everyone faces on a daily basis.

Getting the Right Perspective

[25]"For this reason I say to you, do not be worried about your life, as to what you will eat or what you will drink; nor for your body, as to what you will put on. Is not life more than food, and the body more than clothing? [26]Look at the birds of the air, that they do not sow, nor reap nor gather into barns, and yet your heavenly Father feeds them. Are you not worth much more than they? [27]And who of you by being worried can add a single hour to his life? [28]And why are you worried about clothing? Observe how the lilies of the field grow; they do not toil nor do they spin, [29]yet I say to you that not even Solomon in all his glory clothed himself like one of these. [30]But if God so clothes the grass of the field, which is alive today and tomorrow is thrown into the furnace, will He not much more clothe you? You of little faith! [31]Do not worry then, saying, 'What will we eat?' or 'What will we drink?' or 'What will we wear for clothing?' [32]For the Gentiles eagerly seek all these things; for your heavenly Father knows that you need all these things. [33]But seek first His kingdom and His righteousness, and all these things will be added to you.
[34]"So do not worry about tomorrow; for tomorrow will care for itself. Each day has enough trouble of its own.
- Matthew 6:25-34

Notice that in this passage Jesus deals directly with the problem of worry (which suggests that stress caused by worry is not simply a 21st century problem, people in every generation worried about something) and in dealing with worry He gives us the correct perspective as well as an alternative action in dealing with worry.

A Correct Perspective

The new perspective is found in verses 25-32 and basically it is this:

- Understand that God knows exactly what it is that you need in every area of your life.

- Whether it be food, clothing, work, housing, sex, medical help, family, recreation, etc. God knows, cares and can provide all that you need.

When we look into the future and begin to worry about having the wherewithal to finish a task or the strength to face illness and death, we are taking on a responsibility that belongs to God. He is responsible for the future and has promised to provide the resources to meet that future when it comes. I can be attentive to the future, I can prepare for the future, even be hopeful about the future, however to worry about it is not only futile but sinful because Jesus says, "Do not worry" (verse 25).

Once we have a correct perspective (verse 34, using today's resources to take care of today's needs because God always provides enough today for today) we need an attitude change.

Attitude Change (verse 33)

For those who are over-stressed, the major attitude in their lives is usually that of worry for the future or regret about the past. Jesus explains how things are in the "real" world: God supplies what we need one day at a time. If you do not know this, you end up worrying about having enough, being ok, surviving various challenges in the home, at work or in social situations because you alone have the responsibility to make things happen. However, once you are presented with this fact about God and His providential care, your attitude needs to change from constant worry to humble faith, and your lifestyle goal needs to shift from the acquisition of personal wealth (which provides security) to the development of personal righteousness.

We worry because we think we ourselves are responsible for providing everything. This attitude creates anxiety and burn-out as we focus on acquiring and stockpiling wealth as a way to guarantee our security.

To avoid the over-stress that comes from worry we need to concentrate on God's promise to provide each day what we will need for that day, and change the focus of our lives from creating and maintaining wealth to creating and maintaining a pure conscience before God. This is the true work of a Christian: doing God's will and maintaining a clear conscience in Christ. This means that we will have the normal stress that comes with working at the challenges that face us each day, but avoiding the over-stress produced by the concern that we must do this alone as well as take care of tomorrow's problems today.

Converting Stress into Joy – James 1:2-8

James' approach to worry and stress is to demonstrate that even negative things that happen to us do not have to create the worry that often leads to over-stress and all the negative things that come from it.

> [2]Consider it all joy, my brethren, when you encounter various trials, [3]knowing that the testing of your faith

> produces endurance. [4]And let endurance have its
> perfect result, so that you may be perfect and
> complete, lacking in nothing.
> - James 1:2-4

In verses 2-4 he explains how to short-circuit worry and its negative effects:

- Understand that when trials (and temptations, disappointments, etc.) come your way they can be the cause of some good in life.

- If one meets them with perseverance (patient willingness to bear under) then the constant "perseverance mode" instead of the "worry mode" in us will eventually produce a mature character, and experiencing this mature character (peace, joy, love, patience, kindness, etc.) will be a joyful thing. Wholeness and maturity are what our spirits crave whether we realize it or not (because we are usually distracted by the things of this world).

> [5]But if any of you lacks wisdom, let him ask of God,
> who gives to all generously and without reproach,
> and it will be given to him. [6]But he must ask in faith
> without any doubting, for the one who doubts is like
> the surf of the sea, driven and tossed by the
> wind. [7]For that man ought not to expect that he will
> receive anything from the Lord, [8]being a double-
> minded man, unstable in all his ways.
> - James 1:5-8

In verses 5-8 James explains that doing this is not always easy. However, if one desires to do this but has problems he should ask God for help having faith that God, who provides for each day's needs, will also provide spiritual help for each day's challenges.

Many times, for example, we will not quit a bad habit or attempt to give up a sin which is blocking our spiritual growth because we feel we will never be able to bear an entire lifetime without it. According to the passages we have just studied, God will provide the help we need for today's struggle and will supply what will be necessary for tomorrow's challenge when tomorrow comes. The same strategy works for the help we need to develop our talents, reach our goals or convert our family and friends.

James tells us that trials do not have to be an enemy, producing not only pain and inconvenience but also causing worry and damaging stress in our lives. On the contrary, trials can be used to develop the spiritual maturity we need to produce the peace and joy that are the hallmark of a mature Christian life. Knowing this short-circuits the worry caused by trials.

Summary

The stress that comes from worry is caused by two things:

1. We worry about the responsibility to provide for ourselves.

2. We worry when trials interfere with our efforts to acquire and hoard, which we think will make us happy (by providing security).

The Lord and His earthly brother provide the answer for those who are stressed out because of worry.

1. God will supply what we need each day if we focus our attention on doing His will rather than spending all

of our energies on acquiring and hoarding wealth in an effort to provide security for ourselves.

2. We should not worry about the personal suffering brought about by trials. Instead, we should invest our energies into perseverance when we suffer. If we worry, it will make the suffering worse and accomplish nothing. If, however, we choose to persevere, it will create in us a greater maturity and joy which will not only help us endure the pain but also lower the level of stress caused by that pain.

#2

OVERLY CRITICAL

The word criticism itself is neither positive nor negative - it comes from the basic idea of criterion. A criterion is a standard or principle by which something or someone can be evaluated. For example, in the field of engineering there are certain specifications for a piece of machinery that are used as criterion to judge the quality and value of that part, especially if it is made by different companies. The parts that adhered most closely to the specifications (criteria) would be judged most valuable and having the best quality. In this way, a criterion is the standard against which you measure the value of something or someone.

Defining the problem

Once we understand the idea of criterion, we can put the problem of "criticism" into perspective. Criticism is the judging or evaluating of a person based on certain criteria. There are two forms of criticism:

1. Legitimate criticism

A qualified person makes an informed judgment based on acceptable criteria. For example, a quality control manager examines a product based on manufacturing specifications.

- A teacher corrects a student's assignment on a given subject.
- A parent judges the behavior of a child based on the house rules.
- A journalist analyzes government policies against the impact on society.

There are many examples, but I've chosen a few examples of legitimate criticism to put to rest the false notion that it is always wrong to criticize. Legitimate criticism is necessary; to test the validity of products, ideas, and the behavior of people.

However, to be legitimate, criticism needs to possess three basic components:

A criterion for judgment

For criticism to be legitimate it must use an acceptable standard in its evaluation. You can't judge apples against oranges. Proper criticism needs a consistent and legitimate standard to measure against.

A knowledge of the subject

The more knowedgeable the judge, the more valuable the criticism. Part of the work of "experts" is to offer criticism within their field of expertise in order to raise the level of quality or knowledge.

An unbiased judgment

The most valuable and constructive criticism comes from a knowledgeable and unbiased judge. This is why many companies (especially pharmaceutical) have to send their products to outside companies for evaluation. When criticism contains these basic elements, it serves its purpose which is to separate and evaluate the good from the bad.

The Bible makes reference to legitimate forms of criticism.

> But if we would examine ourselves, we would not be judged by God in this way.
> - I Corinthians 11:31 (NLT)

The first word "examine" is from a Greek word which means to distinguish, or to discern (to evaluate according to a standard = criticize).

The second word translated "judge" means to condemn, as in a court of law.

Paul says that if we criticized our own attitude and conduct in worship carefully, according to the standard of good conduct, we would not be condemned for poor conduct. The point of legitimate criticism is to identify and remove what is lacking and what is flawed, with the goal of restoring to what is best according to an accepted standard.

2. Illegitimate criticism

In our survey I don't think people were concerned about giving or receiving legitimate criticism - I believe the concern was the problem of illegitimate criticism. There are several forms of illegitimate criticism:

Criticism without criterion

This is the most common type of criticism. People criticize without cause, knowledge or standards. They criticize without thinking or basis. Many hide their criticism behind the comment that they're giving an "opinion."

An opinion is simply another word for criticism, but some people think that if they wrap their criticism in an opinion they will not have to take responsibility for what they say.

If you have no knowledge and no standard, it is better to ask questions or remain silent.

> Even a fool when he keeps silent is considered wise.
> - Proverbs 17:28

Criticism without knowledge or criterion is ignorance.

Constant criticism

Some people judge and criticize because that's what they do. Criticism is their main form of communication and expression. It's as if they are compelled to judge and critique every experience they have or person they come in contact with. The problem here is twofold:

1. No one person has enough knowledge to legitimately criticize everything and everyone.

2. These people are mostly negative in their criticism; even in their positive opinions there's always a "but..."

There are times when criticism is needed, but if this is all that one produces, it can't be legitimate. Constant criticism is usually a sign that a person is not happy with themselves, and criticizing everything is a way of deflecting the criticism one feels for oneself.

Condemning criticism

This is the most damaging because it may be based on acceptable standards or the critic may have knowledge and expertise.

The problem is that the judgment/criticism is formed negatively or hurtfully. Since perfection isn't possible, it is easy to always frame our critique in negative ways.

For example, let us look at Simon Cowell, a former judge on American Idol:

- Had knowledge/expertise and qualified to judge.

- His criticisms were mostly framed in negative terms.

- Even his compliments insulted others (best of a bad bunch).

- Negative criticisms often go beyond judging to condemnation and hurt.

Condemning criticism is the type of evaluation that is always framed in negative terms. This is what Jesus refers to in Matthew 7:1-5.

> [1] Do not judge so that you will not be judged. [2] For in the way you judge, you will be judged; and by your standard of measure, it will be measured to you. [3] Why do you look at the speck that is in your brother's eye, but do not notice the log that is in your own eye? [4] Or how can you say to your brother, 'Let me take the speck out of your eye,' and behold, the log is in your own eye? [5] You hypocrite, first take the log out of your own eye, and then you will see clearly to take the speck out of your brother's eye.

Some think this is a command never to judge anything. They think this passage supports the toleration of all kinds of social and moral misconduct. For example, you are wrong if you criticize the gay lifestyle or someone's poor attitude towards others or their work.

But what Jesus is saying is:

Vs. 1-2 – Be careful how you judge, not don't ever judge. You need to be careful because you also will be judged.

Vs. 3-4 – Don't judge with a "log" (negative attitude, ignorance, prejudice) in your eye (your criticism/perception) because this will spoil your ability to judge correctly.

Vs. 5 – First, evaluate yourself and this will enable you to recognize and eliminate your "log" (prejudice, ignorance, etc.) so you can render a fair and accurate criticism.

Negative criticism is justified if it comes from one who is aware of the criterion for judgment, and keeps an eye on himself to make sure the criticism is fair and doesn't become simple condemnation and bullying.

Summary

As Christians we know that criticism is sometimes necessary and, when done correctly, can be quite helpful. We can, however, avoid the temptation to become people who give too much or too negative criticism of others if we remember some simple rules about the use of criticism in general:

1. Use criticism sparingly

No matter how much expertise and insight you have or how fair you are about it - no one likes to receive criticism. There is no rule that says that you have to give your opinion on everything. When it comes to criticism the old saying, "less is more," truly applies. One way to break yourself from the habit of being overly critical is to offer your criticism only under the following circumstances:

- When your criticism will save a person from evil of some kind.

- When your criticism is based on your true expertise, whatever that is.

- When someone actually asks you for your opinion.

Following these rules for the times you offer criticism will greatly reduce those times, and, along with them, the trouble caused by improper criticism.

2. Balance your criticism

Of course there is always something negative you can base your entire judgment on; this is an imperfect sinful world. But the bitter will be so much more palatable if you provide some sweetness to help the medicine go down. Sometimes there is a need to make a judgment call on someone's sin or failure, and you are in the right position to do so.

However, if a ray of hope and encouragement are provided along with the bad, a person is not left feeling completely lost and defeated. All the prophets in the Old Testament, when they were chastising the Israelites for their sins and moral failures, would follow a pattern:

- They would begin by listing the offenses committed.
- Then they would warn of the terrible and sure punishments.
- But they would finish with the promise that God would eventually restore them to a position of hope one day.

Balanced criticism builds the person up because a fair assessment of both the bad and good is made about them when needed. A good rule here is to include two good things for each negative so that the net result is hope for the future from the base of good things now present.

3. Always criticize self first

The best type of critique is the one that has taken a long look at self first. When we do this we tend to be a little more merciful towards others.

> Therefore you have no excuse, everyone of you who passes judgment, for in that which you judge another, you condemn yourself; for you who judge practice the same things.
> - Romans 2:1

Paul says that there is no excuse for the one who criticizes someone else for the things he excuses in himself. Usually when we see ourselves, we are less prone to criticize others; and when we do, we are a little more generous.

4. Realize that Jesus is the true criterion

The problem with criticism, judgment and opinion, especially of others, is that we tend to use ourselves, or our best image of self, or the expectations of others as the criterion/standard for judgment.

If we compare and judge ourselves and others to Jesus as the standard there will be no jealousy, negative envy or false criticism. We all fall short of God's glory and are in need of His mercy.

This attitude creates patience, mercy, kindness, long-suffering and forgiveness towards others. Instead of criticism there is concern. Instead of judgment there is joy that no matter what our failing, all of us have been saved by the blood of Christ.

In the end, when the log is removed from our eye, we see all men as Christ sees them: the objects of His mercy and salvation. If He does not criticize us anymore, we tend to let it go too.

#1

PERSONAL DISCIPLINE

Before we talk about the problems caused by the lack of personal discipline, we should first clearly define what personal discipline is thought to be, and what is really is.

A. General idea of personal discipline

Most people think that personal discipline is the ability to say "no" to our vices and weaknesses. For example, we try to quit smoking and can't so we say, "I lack personal discipline to quit." We overeat, overspend, overdo anything and we chalk it up to lack of personal discipline. So we think personal discipline is this inward ability to resist what is bad for us emotionally, physically and spiritually. To a certain degree this is true but self-discipline is so much more than will power.

B. Biblical idea of personal discipline

In the Bible we have a clear and complete idea of the nature of discipline, both as a virtue possessed and a character trait developed in another.

In the gospel of Mark 5:1-20, the gospel writer describes a man who was totally out of control, one who had lost complete control of self.

> Vs. 1 – They came to the other side of the sea, into the country of the Gerasenes.

The country of the Gerasenes was on the eastern side of the Sea of Galilee across from Jesus' adult home of Capernaum. The Sea of Galilee is not very large, and from one hilltop you can view the neighboring cities and shores.

> Vs. 2-3a – [2] When He got out of the boat, immediately a man from the tombs with an unclean spirit met Him, [3] and he had his dwelling among the tombs.

That a man would live among the tombs made him the worst of outcasts. To touch the dead or their graves made you unclean, to live among them was unthinkable.

> Vs. 3b-4 – And no one was able to bind him anymore, even with a chain; [4] because he had often been bound with shackles and chains, and the chains had been torn apart by him and the shackles broken in pieces, and no one was strong enough to subdue him.

He was insanely strong, untamable, much like a wild beast.

> Vs. 5 – Constantly, night and day, he was screaming among the tombs and in the mountains, and gashing himself with stones.

He was suicidal, in great anguish and living without hope. This man was an example of one who had completely lost the ability to control self and was like a dangerous animal.

> Vs. 6-10 – [6] Seeing Jesus from a distance, he ran up and bowed down before Him; [7] and shouting with a loud voice, he said, "What business do we have with each other, Jesus, Son of the Most High God? I implore You by God, do not torment me!" [8] For He had been saying to him, "Come out of the man, you unclean spirit!" [9] And He was asking him, "What is your name?" And he said to Him, "My name is Legion; for we are many." [10] And he began to implore Him earnestly not to send them out of the country.

Having no self-control doesn't mean that there is no control, it simply means that neither God nor our best selves are in control. In the case of this man Jesus' appearance makes plain that the devil's evil spirits are in full control, and trying to destroy this person with madness.

> Vs. 11-14 – [11] Now there was a large herd of swine feeding nearby on the mountain. [12] The demons implored Him, saying, "Send us into the swine so that we may enter them." [13] Jesus gave them permission. And coming out, the unclean spirits entered the swine; and the herd rushed down the steep bank into the sea, about two thousand of them; and they were drowned in the sea. [14] Their herdsmen ran away and reported it in the city and in the country. And the people came to see what it was that had happened.

Mark describes how the legion of evil spirits, trying to avoid judgment for a time, ask to be sent into the pigs. Jesus permits this, knowing the certainty and outcome of their judgment, and immediately the pigs are destroyed. The country of the Gerasenes was populated by Gentiles which explains the presence of pigs, and it is thought that Jesus uses these to show that the evil spirits were real. The point of these verses however, is that the spirits recognize and immediately submit to Jesus.

> Vs. 15-20 – [15] They came to Jesus and observed the man who had been demon-possessed sitting down, clothed and in his right mind, the very man who had had the "legion"; and they became frightened. [16] Those who had seen it described to them how it had happened to the demon-possessed man, and all about the swine. [17] And they began to implore Him to leave their region. [18] As He was getting into the boat, the man who had been demon-possessed was imploring Him that he might accompany Him. [19] And He did not let him, but He said to him, "Go home to your people and report to them what great things the Lord has done for you, and how He had mercy on you." [20] And he went away and began to proclaim in Decapolis what great things Jesus had done for him; and everyone was amazed.

The important point for us to notice in this section is the part where it says that the demon possessed man was in "...his right mind." That expression is the Bible's way of saying "self discipline." The expression came from two words which meant to save the mind, or to become sound minded.

Now in Mark's account this man's mind was totally lost and out of control. He was naked, living in a cemetery, suicidal, dangerous, crying out like an animal and demon possessed.

He comes to Jesus, and with simply a word the Lord brings the man back to a right mind, a mind controlled, and we see evidence of this: he was dressed, he no longer was prowling about the tombs but seated near Jesus. He was no longer violent, dangerous or incoherent because he appealed to Jesus to return with Him and the Apostles. He received and followed instructions to return home and witness what Jesus had done.

We know he did do this because later in Mark 7:31 Jesus returns to the area and great crowds await Him, and He heals a deaf and dumb man. These people came because of the witness of the demoniac.

In this account Jesus takes a totally out of control man and miraculously restores him to a "right mind' or what we call "self discipline"/"self-control." Obviously, not all lack self-discipline to this degree, and Jesus does not restore all self-discipline miraculously, but in His word we can learn about the providential way God can help us regain the measure of self-discipline we lack or have lost for whatever reason.

Developing Self-Discipline / A Right Mind

So let's review before we go on: self-discipline is not simply self-control, it is a matter of possessing a right mind. The idea is that right actions spring from a right mind. If our minds/hearts are right, the type of actions we desire will follow. Another way of explaining this idea is this:

- Self-discipline as simply self-control is reactionary. Something happens, you react. It is hit and miss, up and down.

- Self-discipline as having a right mind is proactive. You make the good you want happen along with avoiding the bad.

How then, in a non-miraculous way, do we cultivate a "right mind"?

Education

No one is born with self-discipline or a right mind. Education from an early age is the single greatest contributing factor that determines the level of self-discipline we have as adults. This is good news because if self-discipline is learned, it can be acquired throughout one's entire life. Of course it's just easier to learn when taught from an early age. What then must we learn?

A. The True Reality

> [11] For the grace of God has appeared, bringing salvation to all men, [12] instructing us to deny ungodliness and worldly desires and to live sensibly, righteously and godly in the present age, [13] looking for the blessed hope and the appearing of the glory of our great God and Savior, Christ Jesus, [14] who gave Himself for us to redeem us from every lawless deed, and to purify for Himself a people for His own possession, zealous for good deeds.
> - Titus 2:11-14

Paul, the Apostle, summarizes the Christian worldview and encourages his readers to frame their experience, their lives and their perception of the world through this reality. In doing so they will have a "right mind," or the control of self to act in accordance with this reality. For example, knowing this reality will help one not to indulge in reckless pleasure or useless activities that threaten one's soul.

People who give up control of self to allow something else to control them have usually not known the true reality or have abandoned it for some other reality which permits them to cede control of themselves to another person or thing.

B. The True Self

> For through the grace given to me I say to everyone among you not to think more highly of himself than he ought to think; but to think so as to have sound judgment, as God has allotted to each a measure of faith.
> - Romans 12:3

Paul speaks of gifts that God gives to each Christian for service in the church. He also tells us that we need to measure ourselves honestly in light of what God has done for us; no more, no less. He says that we should be "sober minded"/"right minded" when looking at ourselves. The demoniac made no sense to anyone, including himself, until he faced Jesus and confessed that he was in slavery to a legion of devils. No need to explain how or why, Jesus knew, he simply had to confess the truth about self. There is no self-control without self-honesty and self-knowledge. How can you gain control of self if you refuse to acknowledge what it is that now controls you, or where you lack control or a "right mind"?

C. The True Consequences

> [9] Or do you not know that the unrighteous will not inherit the kingdom of God? Do not be deceived; neither fornicators, nor idolaters, nor adulterers, nor effeminate, nor homosexuals, [10] nor thieves, nor the covetous, nor drunkards, nor revilers, nor swindlers, will inherit the kingdom of God.
> - I Corinthians 6:9-10

Sometimes we are deceived by others into thinking we can violate the true reality and survive spiritually and eternally.

Sometimes we deceive ourselves, or we allow what controls us to deceive us into thinking that we can violate the true reality and not suffer the eternal consequences. Because final judgement is delayed, we permit ourselves to be deluded by the momentary pleasure of sin, but in doing so we are not in our right mind. To be in our right mind and thus gain control of self we must keep before us the true rewards and consequences of our actions. This will help us keep all things in their proper and right perspective, and allow a right mind to dictate a proper action.

D. The True Lord

> For who has known the mind of the Lord, that he will instruct Him? But we have the mind of Christ.
> - I Corinthians 2:16

I suppose the biggest problem we face in this exercise of self-control is the word self. The whole idea of having a sound mind, of being of a right mind, is to give over rulership of self to Christ. In the world, the self-help gurus want to get everyone to take charge of their own lives. Self-control through absolute rulership of self by self. Of course this may help with your smoking or eating problems for awhile but it is not a long term solution, and will be disastrous to your soul.

In the true reality our task is to cede control of self to Christ, just like the demoniac did, and allow Him to restore us to a right mind. What I've just explained - the knowledge of the true reality, the true self and the true consequences, is usually what brings us to the knowledge of the only one who can truly be in control of us. When we know these things (by being taught them) we realize that even we cannot be in control of self. This is the great breakthrough in the area of self-discipline or "right mindedness" as the Bible calls it. The great breakthrough is when we give up trying to master self (even for good) and strive to make Jesus the master or the controller of self.

How to Make Jesus the Controller of Self

The last part of this chapter is practical. Just how do we improve self control by ceding control to Jesus? Three things to actually do:

1. Pray. Ask Him to do so! Evangelicals often make the prayer asking Jesus to come into their hearts or to take control, and this is a legitimate request - but not in place of repentance and baptism. Sins are forgiven at baptism (Acts 2:38) not through prayer for Lordship. Jesus said that we should, "seek, ask, knock" Matthew 7:7. People always see this in material terms, asking Jesus for things we need, and this is legitimate, but it also works for intangibles like a request for the Lord to control self and produce a right mind. Pray for this, believing that He hears and answers, and this will become the first step in displacing self and sin as rulers in your life, and making Jesus the king of your soul.

2. Submit. As the Lord takes over there will surely be changes that will happen in your life because of this. You will have to submit to His discipline if you want to cultivate what you call "self-discipline." Sometimes the submission is self-imposed as when you read His word and understand what you must do and simply do it in submission to Him (II Timothy 3:16). Sometimes the submission is imposed by Him through a set of circumstances, restraints or suffering you must endure in order to be perfected (Hebrews 12:4-6). Either way, His sovereignty over you will be felt soon enough, and you will know that you are no longer "in control" and this will become the source of not only your peace but your spiritual power over everything else that once controlled you. I call this freedom through slavery, or mastery through abdication, or self-control through the control of self by Christ.

3. Minister. I go back to our demoniac in Mark 5:20 where Mark writes of him after he left Jesus, "And he went away and began to proclaim in Decapolis what great things Jesus had done for him, and everyone marveled." He didn't let the demons back in. After he called out (prayed) to Jesus and Jesus entered in. After Jesus refused his urgent request to come with Him to which he submitted in obedience without grumbling. What did he do? He went and ministered to his own people. How? Preaching and teaching? No, he had no training, no knowledge. He went and witnessed concerning himself and how Jesus had taken control of him and given him a right mind and how this had changed him. This ministry solidified and perpetuated Christ's position as master.

Without ministry we slip back into our old mode of "self-control" and eventually all the demons make their way back in and the last is worse than the first. Ministry, not perfect self-control, is the way to keep Jesus as Lord of our souls and maintain a "right mind."

Summary

So for one who struggles with self-control issues, it's not about what you take into your body or your mind; it's not what your bodies do or don't do. It's about:

- The true reality you ascribe to
- The true self you acknowledge
- The true consequences you're willing to accept
- The true Lord over you

A change begins with a change of who is Lord over you and is completed when your submission to Him is constant and your ministry in His name is on-going.

#1

BAD EATING HABITS

In this lesson I want to talk to you about habits, especially bad habits and how to break them.

The word "habit" comes from a Latin word which means to "hold" or "live in". A habit is some way of acting, which because of repetition becomes a normal part of our lives. Now we all have habits, all kinds of habits.

Some are good:

- Regular exercise, personal hygiene

- Bible reading and regular church attendance

- Moderate consumption of food, getting lots of sleep etc.

These are the types of things our parents tried to instill in us as young people because they knew that these habits would help us be healthy, happy and productive as adults. Of course, we also have bad habits. Those unhealthy or immoral practices that, because of repetition, have also become habits in our lives. I'm not just talking about the usual bad habits that are evident:

Things like tobacco use or bad language - these are easy to spot and many people feel self-righteous if they've managed to avoid or give up these things in order to please the Lord. There's nothing worse than an ex-smoker preaching at you. There are other bad habits that we have that are more subtle but are as unacceptable as talking dirty, using tobacco or abusing alcohol - you just don't notice them as much.

For example, some people have the habit of wanting their own way all the time; or some people continually talk about others (usually in a negative way). How about people who are stingy - their habit is to make sure they always keep the best part and biggest share for themselves - there's a nasty habit that's not always evident. Then there are people who are busybodies. They can never mind their own business, they have to run everybody's life and everybody's business. It's a habit with them - they always do this if the opportunity presents itself.

I could go on and on about bad habits:

- the habit of making yourself look good
- the habit of giving up too early
- the habit of not telling the whole truth
- the habit of taking the easy way
- the habit of getting angry all the time
- the habit of blaming others for everything
- the habit of feeling sorry for yourself
- the habit of ducking your responsibilities

Do I need to go on? Have I named your bad habit yet?

You see I believe that it's never too late; in fact it's necessary that we develop good habits if we want to live happier more spiritually fruitful lives. Worry, stress, guilt, fear and anger are often the results of negative habits we have cultivated and repeated over the years.

The way to break out of the cycle of worry, guilt and other depressing emotions is to break our bad habits and replace them with habits that will produce greater happiness and satisfaction in our lives.

In this chapter, I want to examine more closely the results of bad habits in our everyday lives and how to overcome them.

Results of Bad Habits

Bad habits have external consequences:

- **Temper** = Conflict/Violence

- **Smoking** = Cancer

There are also internal consequences as well:

1. Feelings of Unworthiness

Continually repeating the same wrong things like:

- losing our temper

- over eat / drink / drugs

- lying to get out of trouble

- lack of sexual control

- giving in to self-pity, depression

Continually repeating these things makes us feel unworthy, that we don't deserve God's forgiveness or His love because we're always repeating the same thing. A lot of people who feel unworthy have a hard time becoming Christians because they think God won't accept them - they're too bad, they have too many bad habits. One of the internal results of a bad habit.

2. Discouragement

Bad habits make us feel paralyzed. We feel helpless because we keep making the same mistakes over and over again - our bad habits are stronger than we are.

3. Defensive

We invent all kinds of methods to avoid dealing directly with our bad habits:

- We'll laugh if off (alcoholics use this).

- Rationalize it (not so bad, others do it, I can control it).

- We get angry if anyone points it out or tries to help us "Don't go there".

- Denial (we run away, deny we have a problem).

- Apathy (I don't care anymore, I can't stop).

These are some of the ways we defend our bad habit - note that none produce peace or happiness; they just enable us to continue with our bad habit.

4. A Rebellious Heart

We decide to keep our bad habit even if it makes us feel bad.

- Even if God forbids it.

- Even if our friends and family and conscience are against it.

At least we're familiar with our bad habit and no one is going to make us change. Of course these feelings of low self-esteem discouragement, defensiveness and anger are not the kinds of things that produce happiness, peace of mind and love.

I suppose that aside from the harm that we do to ourselves with our bad habits, the real tragedy is that we model our bad habits on others and are responsible for introducing and encouraging the same bad habits in other people - sometimes in the ones we love.

Well, I don't want to discourage us so I'll stop talking about the negative side of the story and move to some positive solutions. How do we break the cycle? How do we get rid of bad habits?

1. You have to want to

The Hebrew writer put it this way,

> ...he who comes to God must believe that He is...
> - Hebrew 11: 6

In other words, you must want to believe for faith to be formed in you, no one can force you to believe.

Several months ago a man (not in this congregation) called me about his son. He wanted to know what to do to make his son give up the homosexual lifestyle. We talked for a while and in the end I told him that nothing could be done until the young man wanted to come out of this sinful habit. No amount of preaching, pressure, or nagging can make someone give up a bad habit if they don't want to.

Now someone might ask, "How does a person develop a desire to break a bad habit?" There's no common rule here but from experience I can share with you some things that motivate a person to want to break a bad habit:

A. Truth

When you know the truth about what you are doing and that it is wrong - this may be the spark that gets you going. Sometimes we don't let go because we're not sure that what we're doing is wrong, dangerous or hurtful.

If we can be convinced that the habit is truly a bad one, a sinful one, a hurtful one - this sometimes motivates us to want to break it - that's why parents, family, friends mustn't compromise with what's right when dealing with someone they love who has a bad habit.

B. Love

Love is a great motivator. Sometimes you don't care about the effects of your bad habit on yourself but you care about how it affects others.

- Some give up booze because it's ruining not themselves, but their families.

- Same with tobacco

- Others will go get help for their outbursts of anger because they see the frightened look on the faces of the ones they love.

Those who refuse to break bad habits even with the pleadings of their loved ones really love their bad habits more than they love their loved ones.

C. Pain

Sometimes your bad habit turns around and bites you.

- You get sick because of it.

- You hurt someone because of it.

- You get in trouble because of it.

- You lose your job, your reputation your money, your family because of it.

Some people have to hit bottom (like the prodigal son) before they start dealing with their problems. People who ignore the pain and go on are truly ignorant and rebellious in God's eyes and deserve the condemnation that they will receive.

2. Acknowledge it

If, for whatever reason, you are moved to look for a way out, a way to break your bad habit the next step is to acknowledge it. The hardest thing to do is to acknowledge that we have a bad habit, not just a habit but a bad one. It is difficult to admit that:

- You are a wasteful gambler

- You are impure sexually

- You lack self-control

- You gossip, criticize, are lazy, negative, etc.

It's difficult because you know that when you admit fault, you can no longer participate in it without guilt.

It's difficult because the moment you admit this bad habit and try to leave it you must anticipate a life without a habit you enjoyed - we love our sins (John 3:19).

We'd rather defend our sins or keep our sins than abandon them.

The best to neutralize the power that a bad habit has over us is to shine the light of truth on it by acknowledging exactly what it is and how it is hurting us. (e.g. I am a gossip and because of this I stir up trouble, etc.)

3. Share Your Problem With Another

We confess our sins to God but in order to stay away from them we need help from others. Sharing our burden with someone else (a spouse, another Christian, a trusted friend or family member) creates in us those things we need to deal with bad habits.

For example: sharing our bad habit humbles us and in so doing prepares our souls for God's blessings. He lifts up the humble and brings down the proud (Luke 14:11).

It strengthens our bond with people who can encourage and support us through the times we withdraw from our bad habit. Sharing our problem with another cuts it in half and makes it manageable.

4. Let God Heal You

In the end only God can heal our wounds and make us whole again. We desire to break the habit, we confess it to God and ourselves, we share it with others for support but only God can remove the ache and sinful desire that is at the root of evil. He does this in several ways:

A. He heals you through His Word

As the Centurion said in Matthew 8:8, "..Lord.. speak only your word and my servant will be healed."

God's word sheds the light of truth on our bad habits; it guides us into right conduct and living; it comforts our hearts and convicts our consciences. His word fills the void left by the elimination of the bad habit. If not, it will only be replaced by another bad habit à Smoking à Overeating. This is why regular worship, Bible study and reading leads to a lifestyle that contains less bad habits.

B. Heals through the Holy Spirit

The Bible calls Him the comforter. Paul tells us that we overcome the sin our lives through the power of the Holy Spirit (Romans 8:13). The Spirit of God works directly with our spirit to strengthen us in dealing with our bad habits. You could say the word shows us our faults and the Holy Spirit gives us the strength to do what the word requires of us.

C. Heals through People

If you want to let go of bad habits you need to be with people (Acts 2:42).

- who will not encourage you in evil.

- who are themselves filled with the Holy Spirit.

- who will confront you with the word

- who have overcome the bad habit you're trying to overcome.

You can't get rid of a bad habit in a vacuum you need to draw close to God so He can heal you through His Word, Spirit and the love of His people.

Summary / Invitation

It's easy to shrug off this lesson by saying, "Everybody's got bad habits". The question is, "What about your bad habits?"

- Are you ready to deal with them?

- Are you ready to admit them, share them, give them to God?

We all need to break our bad habits; the problem is when; when will we begin the process? I hope today will be that day for many of us here.

BibleTalk.tv is an Internet Mission Work.

We provide textual Bible teaching material on our website and mobile apps for free. We enable churches and individuals all over the world to have access to high quality Bible materials for personal growth, group study or for teaching in their classes.

The goal of this mission work is to spread the gospel to the greatest number of people using the latest technology available. For the first time in history it is becoming possible to preach the gospel to the entire world at once. BibleTalk.tv is an effort to preach the gospel to all nations every day until Jesus returns.

The Choctaw Church of Christ in Oklahoma City is the sponsoring congregation for this work and provides the oversight for the BibleTalk ministry team. If you would like information on how you can support this ministry, please go to the link provided below.

bibletalk.tv/support

Made in United States
North Haven, CT
08 June 2022